FATE Presents:

Psychic Pets & Spirit Animals

True Stories from the Files of FATE Magazine

1997
Llewellyn Publications
Saint Paul, Minnesota 55164-0383, U.S.A.

FIRST EDITION
Second Printing, 1997

Cover design: Anne Marie Garrison
Book design, layout, and editing: Connie Hill

Library of Congress Cataloging-in-Publication Data
    Psychic pets & spirit animals: true stories from the files of Fate magazine
        p.   cm. (Fate presents)
     ISBN 1-56718-299-2 (pbk.)
     1. Pets—Psychic aspects. 2. Extrasensory perception in animals. 3. Animal ghosts. I. Fate (Chicago, Ill.)
    II. Series.
SF412.5.P79   1996
001.9'4—dc20
                                  95-47294
                                      CIP

Printed in the United States of America

Llewellyn Publications
A Division of Llewellyn Worldwide, Ltd.
P.O. Box 64383, St. Paul, MN 55164-0383

About the FATE Presents Series

Since 1948, FATE magazine has brought true, documented reports of the strange and unusual to readers around the world. For more than four decades, FATE has reported on such subjects as UFOs and space aliens, Bigfoot, the Loch Ness monster, ESP, psychic powers, divination, ghosts and poltergeists, startling new scientific theories and breakthroughs, real magic, near-death and out-of-body experiences, survival after death, witches and witchcraft, and many other topics that will astound your imagination.

FATE has revealed the fakers and the frauds and examined the events and people with powers that defy explanation. When you read it in FATE, you can be sure that the information is certified and factual.

One of the things that makes FATE special is the wide variety of authors who write for it. Some of them have numerous books to their credit and are highly respected in their fields of speciality. Others are plain folks—whose lives have crossed over into the world of the paranormal.

Now Llewellyn is publishing a series of books bearing the FATE name. You hold one such book in your hands. The topic of this book may be one of any of the subjects we've described or a variety of them. It may be a collection of authenticated articles by unknown writers or a book by an author of world-renown.

There is one thing of which you can be assured: the occurrences described in this book are absolutely accurate and took place as reported. Now even more people will be able to marvel at, be shocked by, and enjoy *true reports of the strange and unknown*.

Other Books in the FATE Presents Series

Ghosts, Hauntings & Possessions: The Best of Hans Holzer, Book 1

ESP, Witches & UFOs: The Best of Hans Holzer, Book 2

The Psychic Side of Dreams by Hans Holzer

Extra-Terrestrials Among Us by George Andrews

Poltergeist by Colin Wilson

Contents

Introduction   ix

Animal ESP   1
  The Telling of the Bees   3
  Can Your Dog Read Your Mind?   7
  Lady was a Wonder   13
  Maine's Telepathic Cat   24
  I Owe My Life to a Dog   29
  The Dog Knew   32
  Do Animals Have ESP?   34
  The Mourning Dog   47

Animal Ghosts   51
  Ghost Dog of the Kiamichi Mountains   53
  Little Boy on a Ghost Horse   62
  Limping Ghost of Ballechin   66
  Gef—the Talking Mongoose   72

Animal Magic   85
  Phantom Wolf   87
  The Devil Snakes of Ansuam   92
  I Saw the Spirit of All Animal Life   99

Animal Omens   101
  Banshee   103
  The Raven-Haunted Hapsburgs   109
  A Little Bird Told Me   121
  Amy Castile and the Hellhound   126

Animals and Humans   133
    Psychic Kinship of Man and Beast   135
    The Raccoons Who Came to Dinner   146
    All Things Wild and Lonely   152
    The Kid Must Have Been Dreaming   162
    I Came Back for My Dog   168
    Can Animals Talk to Us?   172

Animals and Life After Death   181
    Are Cats Immortal?   183
    My Beloved Ghosts   189
    The Kitten Came for Phil   195
    Guardian Dog, Guardian Angel   198
    Dog's Love Conquers Death   203

Mystery Animals   207
    Is There a Nandi Bear?   209
    Phantom Panther on the Prowl   221
    Tracking Tasmania's Mystery Beast   230
    Killer Kangeroo   244

Phantom Protectors   247
    Gerigio, the Phantom Dog of Turin   249
    My Guardian Dog that Disappeared   254

Introduction

As the human race grows ever more separated from nature, we are as likely to have close relationships with machines—cars, television sets, stereos, computers—as with animals. The only contact the average late-twentieth-century citizen of Western society has with animals is with a pet, if he or she has one. If not, he or she may occasionally encounter pigeons on a city street, squirrels in a park, or other creatures on an occasional visit to the zoo.

Our neglect of animals is not exactly benign. Whole animal species vanish almost daily as human beings destroy their habitats, poison their (and our) air and water, or hunt or poach them to extinction. It seems not to have occurred to anybody, except a few mystics, philosophers, and "environmental extremists," that other species may have just as much a right to exist—and to exist in dignity, free from exploitation—as we do.

Yet, strangely, for all our science, for all that biology and medicine have learned about living things, some of the most important questions about animals remain unanswered: Can animals think? How aware are they of their own existence (one way of asking if they have souls)? How do they communicate? Can they communicate with us? What is the nature of animal intelligence?

Beyond such basic mysteries are deeper questions most scientists are not ready to ask, but which a large body of human testimony compels us to raise: are some animals, like some people, psychic? If human beings survive death, do animals too? Are there bonds that exist between people and animals that are beyond our ability to comprehend, even in light of the possibilities suggested by parapsychology?

The articles and stories that follow tell us how little we know, even about the animals we think we know best. They also suggest that animals are, in many ways, more like us than we think—and that, like us, they sometimes step over into the strange and unknowable realm of the paranormal, where all things, or nearly all things, are possible.

Animal ESP

Extrasensory perception is almost always thought to be something that occurs only between human beings because only human beings, with their advanced consciousness and mental complexity, possess it. Like so many other things that "everybody knows," this isn't true either—and it's not just the higher animals that have ESP. Take insects, for example ...

The Telling of the Bees

Ruby Parker
March 1964

Telling the bees is an old New England custom. According to this custom, when someone dies the bees must be told at once and their hives draped in black; otherwise they will fly away and hive somewhere else.

John Greenleaf Whittier wrote this poem:

Telling The Bees

Before them, under the garden wall,
    Forward and back,
Went, drearily singing, the chore girl small
Draping each hive with a shred of black.

It was a chilly, blustery day in February 1959, in southeast Missouri. Gray clouds hanging low in the sky seemed almost to brush the bare trees. It was the bleak day of my father's funeral.

My father, Charles D. Hitt, was a small farmer who lived in the gently rolling hills near Moreley, Scott County, Missouri. He raised many cantaloupes and watermelons—and kept bees. Someone had told him many years ago that bees somehow helped the melons, and Dad had become very much attached to his bees.

3

He seemed to have some kind of a working arrangement with his bee friends, and they, in turn, seemed to sense his love and affection. He could handle his bees, work with them, walk about the area where the hives were stationed, row on row, and never once was he stung. The rest of us always kept our distance. Let one of us venture too close and we invariably paid the penalty! Our relationship with Dad's bees through the years had consisted primarily of enjoying breakfasts of hot pancakes with butter and honey, and there our relationship ended.

After Dad's sudden death of a heart attack, which he suffered at home, his body was taken to a funeral home some twelve miles distant.

At one o'clock, the day of the funeral, we all were at Dad's farmhouse. Suddenly, above the small talk of visiting friends and kin, we heard the buzzing of Dad's bees. Bees active in mid-winter? Impossible!

The time came for us to leave for the church and for our last goodbye to Dad. As we got into our cars in the driveway, the bees were flying here and there in the strangest manner.

Did they know their master was close by in our small town church?

Dozens of bees buzzed over our heads, and one or two lit gently on our hands and faces as if to caress us in our sorrow. We wondered and drove away.

The funeral service for Dad was held at the church and a short graveside service followed in Forest Hills Cemetery. As the family assembled under the graveside canopy, we noticed several bees in the profusion of flowers. Many things raced through my mind. I recalled our morning's breakfast table conversation and my casual question, "I wonder whether Dad's bees will swarm today as it says they will in the old English legend?" and my husband's calm assurance that the bees would not swarm—not in mid-winter. "They're hibernating," he had explained. But the bees were there!

Later, sometime after the ceremony and after the flowers had been nicely arranged, the family returned to the cemetery. As we neared the grave, my sister came running down the hill very much excited.

"The bees are coming in great masses," she cried.

The funeral director, the sexton, and others who were still in the cemetery watched with us as the bees came toward us "in a beeline." A great black cloud of them flew directly from our home across the valley. They covered every blossom on the flower-bedecked grave. They crawled over our faces, our arms, and our hands, and yet they did not sting any of us assembled there at the grave. I felt like the prophets of old must have felt as they witnessed the miracles of the Master. I could almost hear Him say, "Peace be with you. Be not afraid."

When we returned home, we were met by my younger brother. He was as excited as we. "Dad's bees are acting up," he said, "the older bees are leaving the hives by the hundreds—and they are not coming back." And they did not return.

Perhaps the bees were somehow following an ageless urge to join their friend. Miracle, extrasensory perception, or whatever, a great tranquility descended over our house in the gently rolling hills that evening. We gathered on the back porch of the house for one last glimpse of the countryside before returning to our respective homes. The setting sun broke through the overcast sky for a moment, and we carried with us the picture of Forest Hills in the distance, bathed in the weak winter sunlight. We all were thinking about the "miracle of the bees."

Can Your Dog Read Your Mind?

Hattie Chesney
August-September 1951

Many tales are told of the psychic abilities of animals during great stress, but I wonder how many people are aware of the daily telepathic messages which pass between themselves and their pets. Some dogs seem to be particularly telepathic. The owners of good hunting dogs will bear this out with instances in which dogs have responded above and beyond ordinary expectations to cues and signals.

Is this telepathic bond, this rapport, the reason why the dog, alone of all animals, has remained the steadfast companion of man?

My own experiences with the telepathy of dogs began in early childhood. My father owned a large Airedale named Bruno. He often demonstrated as a parlor trick the ability of Bruno to hear him mentally. Bruno slept in the dining room. He slept heavily, for he was very active during the day. Yet he never failed to answer immediately, out of a sound sleep, when my father would say in his mind, "Come here, Bruno." My father performed this trick many times in groups of different friends. Bruno always came. Yet if he were called by voice, he would awake only after several loud calls. Apparently this telepathy worked both ways between my father and Bruno. Bruno swallowed a sponge rubber ball and spent several weeks in the veterinary hospital. Although reports stated he was recovering, my father was obsessed, one night, with a necessity for seeing him. He went to the hospital at 1 A.M. and frantically begged admittance from the night watchman. The man refused, saying that he had just looked at the dog and that he was perfectly all right. They argued for half an hour, my father declaring that he could hear Bruno howling. Finally the night watchman locked the door and my father was forced to leave. In the morning we were informed that Bruno was dead.

My father brought his body home and, because of the frozen ground, could not bury it for several days. During this time I was unable to sleep soundly because of the constant rattling of Bruno's collar and leash which hung on a nail in the hall. During his life Bruno had had the habit of going to his collar and shaking it when he wanted to be taken for a walk. After he was buried, the noise stopped.

After Bruno died, we did not have a dog for several years. My father jokingly stated that the soul of Bruno would not allow it. Remembering the rattling collar, I wondered if he was joking.

Our dogs after that were intelligent but did not seem to be particularly telepathic. The only phenomenon which I remember was on my own part. Shortly after I was married, my husband and I acquired a nice dog named Pal. We had him for only a few months when, sitting at the dressing table, I was suddenly overcome by an overwhelming sadness and burst into tears. My husband asked why I was crying and I said, "Pal is going to die." He replied, "That is ridiculous: Pal is in

8

perfect shape," but within two months Pal was dead from rabies.

Shortly after that we acquired Storm, a Great Dane. Once out of his puppyhood, Storm displayed some very unusual telepathic powers. Every day, precisely two minutes before my husband arrived home from work, Storm would arise from his bed in the back of the house, yawn, stretch, and go to the front window to greet my husband. This may not seem unusual, since many dogs have an accurate sense of time, but if my husband stopped for any reason and was late, Storm still did not arise until two minutes before his arrival. When my husband went into the army, Storm did not make the mistake of waiting for him to come home evenings.

One night, when I had not taken Storm for a walk in such a long time that he had ceased to beg for one, I sat down in a chair, thinking, "As soon as I have rested I will take Storm for a walk." The thought had no sooner left my head when Storm came dancing in from the room where he had been sleeping, and began to frolic back and forth between me and his leash. He plainly showed that he knew what I intended and wanted to hasten the process.

I was never able to bathe this dog or give him medicine without his knowing about it in advance. I would try to keep the thought of my intentions from my head, but the minute that the idea occurred to me Storm would give me a look that plainly said, "traitor," and slink away to hide under the bed.

One year we gave Storm some schooling under the direction of an animal trainer who lived about two miles from our house. I took Storm there one afternoon, preceding my husband who was to follow us in a couple of hours. Storm went through his paces nicely, returning to his stool after each trick. Suddenly his mind seemed to leave us; he would only face in the direction of home and wag his tail. He did not seem to hear my commands and I grew angry. "Let him alone," said the animal trainer, "I think your husband has left the house and he knows it." Sure enough, in exactly the allotted time necessary to cover the distance, my husband pulled up. After greeting him Storm acted naturally again.

Among our neighbors and relatives were several who were mentally deranged. Storm's reaction to these people was violent: they threw him into a state of near-hysteria. He was a perfect barometer of insanity; borderline cases bothered him only slightly, but he was almost driven into a fit by some [people] who had been confined in institutions and dismissed as incurable, but harmless. The hair rose on his neck and he walked stiff-legged and gingerly around them as though he were treading on eggs.

He would never allow them to touch him and during the time such people were in the house he was never still, emitting constantly a noise which was combined bark, whine and howl. I have often wondered if the profusion of delta waves, said by scientists to radiate from the brains of the insane, was the cause of his strange actions. To no other people did he behave in this fashion, although drunkenness infuriated him.

Storm was very fond of pears and, during the season, would eat one or two pears each day from the pear tree behind the house, but on the day that my grandfather was to arrive to pick the pears Storm would eat several dozen and bury a quantity for future use. Year after year he did this. How could he know that my grandfather was coming to take the pears?

Storm had an old shoe as a plaything. He tired of it quickly and did not play with it often. We kept it in the children's toy box along with their toys, getting it out only on rare occasions. One day, during the shoe rationing (during wartime), I was studying the ration coupons, trying desperately to make the remaining coupons provide us all with shoes. Shoes, and shoes alone, were on my mind. Storm sat in front of me, during this time, staring at me intently.

After about fifteen minutes he left, and I heard him rooting in the toy box. Afraid that he might chew up some of the children's toys, I called, "Storm, get out of there." He came in proudly with his shoe and dropped it in my lap. Although I tried to get him to play with it he would not. Each time I gave it to him he dropped it back in my lap. Did he see those visions of shoes in my head and feel my desire for shoes?

On the night before Storm died, he was unduly affectionate. I was sitting in a chair, stretched out with my legs up on a stool. He climbed completely into my lap, quite an accomplishment for a dog of his size. The next night, when he wanted to go out at midnight I scolded him for wanting to be let out so late. He gave me a most peculiar look, wise and almost saucy. He was shot by a fanatic neighbor that night and I never saw him alive again.

I remembered that look. I was to see it again on the face of a pet cat, a year later. I have noticed it since on other animals as they go out for the last time. It is a knowing look, almost merry. The translation seems to be, "You mean well, but you don't know what I know." I like to think that our animals are fully aware of their coming deaths and go to meet them without resentment, expecting something better to come afterward.

None of our dogs has ever howled before its death (the exception being Bruno, who apparently sensed the presence of my father). However, our present dog, Mister, howled every evening for a week before he had a nearly fatal accident, though he usually never howls.

Of course, every one is familiar with the howling of dogs upon a death in the family. Blackie, my grandfather's cocker spaniel, howled constantly at the time of the death of a member of the family who was vacationing 500 miles away. The dog stopped her howling as soon as the message of the accidental death arrived.

Occasions such as this are frequently observed. It is the everyday communication which we would like to have noticed. Watch your own dog. Doesn't he often seem to know things which his five senses could not have told him? My dogs have proved to me conclusively that there is a telepathic link between dogs and their masters.

Lady was a Wonder

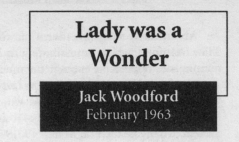

Jack Woodford
February 1963

I first heard of "Lady" years ago in a fan letter I got from England, from an English writer named Shaw Desmond. He wished to know what I thought of Lady. Although I lived in Richmond, five miles from Lady at the time, I never had heard of her.

I hate horses. Next to politics they constitute the most vicious racket in America. Besides, they bite, kick, stink, and are inclined to knock your eye out with their tails when they switch flies. In this frame of mind, I approached Lady.

I never found out about Lady, although my investigation covered a period, off and on, all told, of about thirty years. Dr. J. B. Rhine also investigated Lady and never found out about her. Her owners never did. Psychologists, psychiatrists, educators, priests, ministers, rabbis who came from all over the world to have a look at Lady never found out about her either.

Hollywood tried in vain to import Lady. Her owners would have no part of it. The owners, Mr. and Mrs. C. D. Fonda, never made any money out of Lady. They were simple, country, "God-Fearing" people. They never exploited Lady. They never put up so much as a neon sign to point out Lady's location on Ruffin Road between Petersburg and Richmond, Virginia.

About thirty years ago I went out to see Lady for Shaw Diamond, whose novels in England got excellent reviews and, respectably enough, not much money.

I had a dickens of a time finding Lady. When I did I saw a swayback, tattered horse who looked old. Nobody seemed to know how old she was, even though, when she died on March 19, 1957, the papers said she was thirty-three years old. If this is true, then she was eight when I saw her. She looked older.

She was in a small yard with a tumble-down fence. She had a leaky roofed old stable. The house of the owners was a small house and they never moved from it. The whole aspect was one of poverty. Hollywood would have paid the Fondas $100 grand at any time and it cost me a quarter to interview Lady.

She was the most loathsome-looking horse I have ever seen, before or since, and I detested her and was enraged with Shaw Desmond for getting me into such a mess of mud.

The horse looked me squarely in the eyes. I avoided her gaze, but I could feel—and Mrs. Fonda told me—that Lady had taken an instant dislike to me, a dislike which increased through the years. This was mutual.

"Do you want to come inside?" the woman asked.

We went into an untidy stable, where there was a curious contraption with the alphabet on it. It looked as though it had been bought second-hand from a vaudeville animal act. If the horse nosed one of the letters it stood up.

Lady was brownish, mottled and spotted. The woman was unfriendly. The horse hated me. I hated the horse. The surroundings were most uncongenial. There was no place to sit.

"What do you want to ask the horse?" Mrs. Fonda asked me.

"What's my name?"

The horse knocked down four letters: "J-A-C-K."

I nearly fainted. The lady couldn't possibly have known who I am, if anybody. I was dressed in nondescript fashion; my hair was uncombed. I looked worse than the horse. I had made up my mind to go see the horse only half an hour before, and I'd never even heard of her before that.

When I recovered I snarled, "That's not my name." (And it isn't! Not really!)

I figured the horse was trained to knock down common names like Jack and Dick, and if it made a mistake the woman would doubletalk the horse out of it somehow.

The woman gave me a suspicious look. The horse gave me a contemptuous one. The woman said to the horse, "Try again."

This time the horse knocked down four more letters: "J-O-S-H."

I asked the woman, "Is there a chair here?"

I honestly felt dizzy. The woman grudgingly brought me a chair. I sat down. I tried to collect my thoughts. The name I am usually called is "Jack," although it is not my name. Only one person on this earth ever called me "Josh," my grandmother, since that is what she affectionately made out of "Josiah," my legal first name. My grandmother was dead.

For some reason I was shaking all over, as though I'd seen a ghost.

"What's the matter," the woman asked, "are you sick?"

15

"I guess so," I told her.

She showed no sympathy, and what she now told me, she told me many other times in later years: "Lady wants you to leave."

Lady was knocking her front foot on the floor. And Lady didn't want me to leave one-tenth of one percent as much as I wanted to leave.

I got up and went out. Far off I could hear the traffic on the Dixie Highway. It was a comfortable city sound. Born in the middle of Chicago, I am always disoriented in a small place.

I went out to the car and sat there and tried to think like an intellectual. There was bound to be some explanation I told myself, but coincidence, chance, none of those would fit—not with those two names, Jack and Josh. It occurred to me that Shaw Desmond might have tipped off the woman and described me, or some such, but that wouldn't fit because Desmond didn't know about Josh, nor did anybody in the whole state of Virginia. Not even my daughter knew about that; nor my wife.

So I thought of the British Society for Psychical Research and I thought of the theories of telepathy, with no pleasure whatever. I don't believe in telepathy from one human mind or animal mind to another. I think there is something there, but I don't know what it is. Eventually I felt better and drove home.

I never told Shaw Desmond a thing about it. I never told anybody anything about it—until this minute.

When you interviewed the horse you stood close enough to it to touch it easily.

There were no props of any kind. The stable was just a stable. There was nothing in it (except the board on which the horse could knock down answers) that wouldn't be found in any ordinary stable. There were several windows. There was bright light. You could see under and over and all around the horse. I watched the woman out of the corner of my eye (when I went back there again later). She had no possible connection with the horse. She yelped orders at it if it were dilatory. Otherwise she said nothing, did nothing. She'd look off out the window with an abstracted expression. Her feet were motionless on the floor. Nobody else was in or around the stable. There was nothing under it, nothing over it. Her hands remained motionless; her body remained motionless. Her breathing was regular. She seldom even looked at the horse. There were no sounds of any kind, only dead stillness.

I discussed this from time to time with various vaudeville people who were acquainted with animal acts. We considered the whistles that can't be heard by the audience, all that sort of thing. Two of these experts, who I knew, went out there to have a look. They told me they couldn't for the life of them figure out how it was done. They were enormously impressed.

Chiefs of Police consulted the horse concerning crimes. They were always reporting to the newspapers that the horse solved the crimes.

Numerous persons told me that the horse was bewitched, but they would never tell why they thought so. I suppose they couldn't without exposing family skeletons.

Finally, one day I found Mrs. Fonda outside raking leaves. "How do you account for it?" I asked her.

She looked up at me wearily, "I don't know."

"Do you consult the horse about your life?"

"Of course not. I consult God."

"Then doesn't it seem to you passing strange to let other people take what would appear to be a rather faithless attitude toward their own destinies and God by consulting the horse?"

"If God didn't want it, it couldn't happen."

I was tempted to ask why not, considering some of the things that would appear to be fairly inimical to God that did happen, but I remained silent and she added, "God has let Lady live a happier and a longer life than I ever heard of any other horse doing."

"How old is Lady?"

"I don't know."

"How old do you think she is?"

"I have no idea."

You will think (and so have I) of lots of other things I could have asked her, but this woman was a bit irascible naturally, and she had been plagued by questions for decades. I knew she viewed me with some antipathy, because all Lady had to know was that my car was coming down the road to start being intractable.

Often, when I was waiting my turn to get in, or after I had come out, I talked to people standing around. Many of these people had been coming for years; one of them from Saskatoon, Saskatchewan, Canada. These people had heard about Lady through articles in newspapers and magazines written by people who had visited Lady. These articles usually made preposterous claims. The woman in charge of Lady never did. Confronted with some of these tales, she always said they were not true or they were exaggerated.

However, some claims she would substantiate. Natives from around the South came to consult the horse about illnesses. I heard that the horse often made some simple diagnosis that would turn out to be accurate as later proved clinically. Mrs. Fonda recited one of these and gave me the doctor's name. I called him up. He confirmed it.

The local papers never went overboard about the horse, but they often reported cases of lost persons being located by the horse. Mrs. Fonda confirmed these reports, and several locations occurred at times when I was in Richmond. I checked on three of them. All three reports tended to show something supernatural or preternatural had occurred.

I didn't see Lady or her mistress again for ten years. By that time I supposed the phenomenon, whatever it was, would have been exposed somehow. It wasn't. It was going stronger than ever. I checked Lady's mistress carefully until I had satisfied myself she was obviously incapable of trickery of any kind about anything, with anything. Whatever it was went on between her and this confounded nag, she thought God did it.

Soon after that I left Richmond again, still unable to put the horse out of my mind.

When I returned to Richmond to stay briefly another 10 years later, I got a letter from a minor official in Washington who told me he would be down for one day, for one purpose only: to see Lady, the Wonder Horse. He wanted me to fix it. I explained to him there was no fix necessary so far as I knew (I hadn't seen the horse since coming back), and that Richmond was not a place where everything had to be angled.

So he came on down one morning with his pretty wife.

There was still nothing identifying the farm but a nondescript wooden sign, practically unnoticeable from the Dixie Highway. The sign was weatherbeaten; the road to the corral was dirt, very narrow and uncomfortable to negotiate. Nothing was changed. We were the only visitors.

I wanted no part of the horse and I knew the horse wanted no part of me. When the Washingtonians saw the set-up, they lost some of their interest. How could anything that wasn't expensive be any good? I sat outside while they went in to interview the horse.

But I was extremely uncomfortable. I had a hunch something was going to happen. I hadn't wanted to go; now I wished I hadn't. The farm was small. There were no other stock except dejected-looking poultry. You couldn't see any other house from there, just trees and rolling country. Virginia creeper vines ran all over everything.

Now out came the Washington visitors, into the car. They said nothing, not a word.

As I drove back toward Richmond, I forced conversation about other matters, since apparently they didn't want to talk about the horse, and I didn't either. Evidently they'd had a rough time. I knew that Lady's mistress could be plenty rough with people she didn't like. Now my guests wanted to catch an earlier train that they had planned on back to Washington.

At the Broad Street Station, I started to go into the station with them but the woman went on ahead without saying goodbye and the man detained me.

"It was damn cute of you," he said, "to tell the Old Bag to tell the horse all about us. I suppose you did it because you wanted us to have a good show ... but I don't think it was so damn funny to tell her we aren't married!"

Then he walked off.

I stood there, stunned. I had told the horse on them? How would I know they weren't married? I didn't know anything at all about the woman, and all I knew about the man was that, like everybody else in Washington, he wanted to write a novel exposing Washington.

I got to wondering, in savage, manic-depressed fashion, what was the worst they could do to you for shooting a horse in Virginia, and drove home so deep in thought that I could have gotten killed in traffic.

Louella, my daughter, had wanted terribly to go see the horse when she knew I was taking them, but had decided against it since it would mean missing school.

I had promised to take her tomorrow, and I never broke a promise to Louella in my life! She adored horses and every other living thing. After a rain it was hell to walk down the street with her, being careful not to step on worms that had come up for a bath.

I tried to trade Louella out of it, but it was strictly no deal.

"Remember one thing," I finally cautioned her. "The horse will have seen the *Sunday Times Dispatch*. Your picture was in it. It says you're thirteen, and an arrived novelist. It says you're Welsh. It says a lot of things."

"I won't ask the horse anything it could possibly know. I'll ask it things neither you nor mother nor anybody else on earth could know but me."

"Good ..." I said grimly.

Saturday turned out to be the angelic sort of day Richmond has once a year, New York has twice a year, some years, and Hollywood has every day. I drove Louella out, parked as far away as I could get, and let her make it alone.

Although she was only thirteen, she already had sold poetry, articles, and short stories to magazines, besides having a novel published. In her entire life I never had seen her anything but happy and ebullient.

But she came back from her visit to the horse looking as though she had been stabbed. Her eyes were wet. I could see that she was near tears, so I didn't speak to her. I sat and drove in silence, morosely trying to think of ways to assassinate a horse without getting caught at it.

Later Louella said, "It's the only horse I ever saw that didn't like me. It didn't like me one bit. It kept pawing the floor. I asked it a question mentally."

"What question?"

"About the wish."

It was no use to ask her about the wish. Since she was nine every time she saw an early star she made the same wish.

"What did the miserable creature say?" I asked.

"It kept on saying nonsense until the lady spoke severely to it and then it said 'No.'"·

"Surely you don't think the horse is psychic?" I said.

"All animals are psychic. So are all human beings when they are very young. Somebody tells us it's all nonsense, and then we no longer believe it and we're no longer psychic," Louella said.

"What was the nonsense the horse said?"

"Josh."

I pulled myself up. "How did it come to write 'Josh?'"

"I don't know. It started writing it right away when I came in. It puzzled the lady too, and made her mad. She was nice to me, but she got mad at the horse. I don't ever want to go there again. I felt queer."

"You didn't feel any queerer than I did," I told her grimly. "I'll never go near that animal again either."

"Why should an animal hate me?" she wanted to know. "I love all animals. They usually know it."

"It wasn't you it hated. It apparently knew I was with you; and it hates me because it knows I hate it."

Eventually, many years later, she told me what "the wish" was. She had asked the horse that day: "Will my father and I die at the same time?"

The real reason I never have written an article about Lady before is that I always had to ask myself before I wrote the article: "What do you believe about this?"

I still don't know.

But I can tell you one thing about Mrs. Fonda. I know, beyond the shadow of a doubt, that what always worried her was that she believed any horse could do what Lady did, and she never could understand why other people didn't go get an alphabet and a horse and prove it. She never saw anything in the least unusual about the phenomenon. It didn't even interest her.

Her friends, too, thought that any horse could do it, but they considered it irreligious to encourage such goings on. They thought people should go to God with their problems, not to a horse.

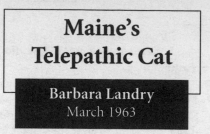

Maine's Telepathic Cat

Barbara Landry
March 1963

It was nearing midnight and bright moonlight on July 21, 1962, when William and Mina Miles returned to their home on North Elm Street in Yarmouth, Maine, after an evening out. The couple were in especially good spirits, because Bill Miles had just concluded a tour of sea duty aboard the U.S. Destroyer Tills with the U.S. Navy Reserve. They had, in fact, attended a party of the ship's company in the nearby city of Portland.

En route to Yarmouth, they stopped to pick up their three-and-one-half-year-old daughter, Selina, whom they had left at the home of a baby sitter. As the three approached their driveway, the headlights from the car picked up an inanimate object in the middle of the road. It was so small they almost ran over it. Mrs. Miles uttered a cry, for it was a light-colored animal closely resembling the family cat, Streaky, who had given birth to four kittens only the week before.

Bill Miles stopped the car and got out. "Sure enough," he said, "it was Streaky." She apparently had been hit by a passing motorist some time during the evening. She was dead. The cat had wanted to go out when the couple left the house at 7:30 P.M. that same evening. Some time in the interim she had been killed.

24

Gently Bill lifted the body of the white feline onto the grass. After getting his wife and daughter settled, he took the mother of the newborn kittens out behind the house where he laid her under a bush. When daylight came he would bury her.

As he walked back to the house he wondered if the same fate had befallen their other cat, four-year-old Hoppy, the mother of Streaky. About the middle of May, two months ago while he was away on sea duty his wife had written that Hoppy had disappeared. No one in the neighborhood had seen her since. Bill wondered if she too had been a "hit and run" victim and had crawled into the nearby woods to die.

But Bill Miles had other problems—four in fact. What was he to do with the orphaned litter? Should he dispose of the four kittens? Or could he and his wife possibly hand-feed them for the next few weeks? Caring for the litter seemed an insurmountable task to the Navy reservist, and to his wife, who was expecting a second child shortly. With this thought in mind, both slept fitfully.

On the same Saturday night, in another house, about a mile away, another cat nursed her brood of five kittens. According to the diary kept by Naida Nixon, wife of Milton A. Nixon of North Road, the brown tabby had delivered her babies June 23. She had "just appeared" at their home around the middle of May.

"She just seemed to move in," said Mrs. Nixon, much to the delight of 10-year-old Kathy Nixon and her twin sisters, Kaye and Carol, who were teenagers.

The cat almost never left her kittens, now four weeks old, the Nixons reported. She had given birth in the closet in Kathy's room, and only two or three days before the whole feline family had been moved into an attached shed where the mother cat continued to be a most attentive and devoted mother.

However, on this particular night, July 21, she was restless and unhappy. About 9:00 P.M. she began to scratch and meow as if to attract the attention of the Nixon family, ignoring the cries of her young. The family retired about 11:30 P.M. By early morning her caterwauls had increased, and at 6:00 A.M., the Nixons finally let her out the back door. She disappeared behind the barn.

On Sunday morning, Bill Miles awoke thinking of the fate of the week-old kittens in the basement of the house. He got up to check on them. When he reached the bottom of the cellar stairs he was startled to see the shadow of a cat through the cellar window! And then he shouted to his wife, "Hey, it's Hoppy!" For the cat on the windowsill was none other than their four-year-old Hoppy, mother of Streaky. She had been gone from the Miles house almost two months. Now, here she was, back.

Bill let Hoppy into the cellar. He also noticed happily that she recently had had kittens of her own and would have milk for the orphaned litter! It was too good to be true. By this time the week-old kittens were crying noisily. It had been more than twelve hours since Streaky had left her family, never to return.

Grandmother Hoppy, running in the direction of the noisy babies, sniffed briefly and climbed into the box with the four kittens.

Both Bill and Mina Miles stared in utter amazement.

Back at the Nixon home, ten-year-old Kathy was becoming more and more upset over the continued absence of the mother cat from her own family. The Nixons banded together and combed the acreage around their Cape Cod farmhouse. They called and called, but to no avail. They had practically given up, when from behind the barn the cat appeared, pursued by a strange man, who was running and breathlessly shouting, "That's my cat, that's my cat!"

Hoppy was well in the lead, and she made a bee line for the shed and her kittens!

Bill Miles, with his urgent need to have Streaky's orphaned litter continue to be fed, had felt he must follow the grandmother cat on her return to her own kittens. He figured they must be hidden somewhere in the woods, and into the woods Hoppy led her former master. He followed her through a maze of trees and brush, over fields, and around thickets and scrub oak.

"I lost her a couple of times," Miles recalls.

He finally came into the clearing behind the Nixon's house, still chasing the mother cat, and that is when Naida Nixon recorded in her diary, "Mr. Miles found the cat and the five kittens."

In order that all nine kittens should survive, Kathy and her family consented to move Hoppy's litter to the Miles' cellar. There was only one stipulation: one of Hoppy's kittens would one day return to live with the Nixon family.

The Nixons and the Miles still shake their heads in puzzlement when relating this strange story. They can't help wondering how Hoppy knew her daughter had died, leaving an orphaned and hungry litter of kittens at her former home. It is possible to wonder, also, where Hoppy got her strong sense of responsibility. The daily newspapers are full of the sad stories of human babies less well cared for. Hoppy had started acting strangely during the evening on which her daughter actually was killed, perhaps at the exact moment the other cat had lost her life!

But how could this cat, who had not been near her former home since the month of May, possibly have known that her daughter had been killed and had left behind a litter of kittens that needed nursing?

Answer? Anyone?

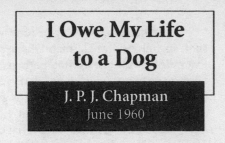

I Owe My Life to a Dog

J. P. J. Chapman
June 1960

Most people, at some time or other, have had such narrow escapes from death that seconds were of vital importance. Personally, I have had quite a few narrow squeaks; my most memorable escape I owe to a dog.

It happened in late October 1918. I was a mechanic in an Air Squadron. The Germans were in heavy retreat. I was sent, with some other men, to an advance emergency landing ground behind Cambrai. There were perhaps twenty-five of us in all. Extra hands in the cook house worked on a rotational basis. Eventually, of course, my turn came.

The cook house was nothing more than a knock-up tin shanty, one end open, where one got boiled on one side and frozen on the other.

The squadron had picked up a hungry mongrel some months before. He was such a lovable dog that he was unofficially "put on the strength." Naturally, he knew what was good for him and spent most of his time in the cook house—unless he was fighting with some interloper who wanted to muscle in.

Snuffer, as he was soon named because of his favorite activity, selected a few personal friends. I was honored to be one of these.

The emergency landing ground was rather a hot spot, in full view of German Observation "Sausages" five miles in front of us. But, perhaps as no effort had been made to put up a "show," Jerry left us alone.

On my day in the cook house as general factotum, helping the so-called cook, about two miles on the other side of the German lines Jerry had a long range gun. It was our job to spot and, if possible, put it out of action. This gun was not fired at any particular target, but shells were lobbed over at various points in the hope of a "hit." At about 11:00 A.M. a couple of shells burst a quarter of a mile away.

"Cor! Blimey!" remarked our Cockney cook. "Gettin' a bit 'ot ain't it, mate?"

I said there was consolation in the fact that the one that had our number on it we would never hear!

Shortly after this, our dog got restless, walking around the boilers, in and out of the shed, and generally acting fussy. Finally, he sat down and started to howl like a forlorn wolf.

"Well, strike me pink! Wot's the matter with the dawg ter day?" asked the cook.

"Seems to me," I replied, "he knows something we don't."

After about five minutes of steady howling the dog got up and went over to the cook and turned around and around his legs. A few moments later Snuffer came over to me and started barking furiously. I bent down to stroke him, wondering what it was all about. No sooner did I put out my hand than the dog took it in his mouth—very gently—and gave every indication that he wanted to get me out, that I should come away with him.

I looked at the cook and said, "Here, come on, Bill. He's got a line somewhere. Let's follow. The grub won't be any more spoilt for a while."

The dog let go of my hand and we followed him to a shell hole about twenty-five yards from the cook house. In we went. After we were there some few minutes Bill thought he would go. The dog immediately became quite fierce, showed his teeth, and growled. Bill sat back down. Snuffer subsided.

It was not too bad in the hole, protected from the nasty wind. We had some fags, so we smoked away the time. After a few minutes more Snuffer looked up at the sky, then looked at me. Immediately we heard a whine and then a terrible crash. A shell had hit the cook house right plumb in the middle. Bill and I sat just looking at each other. After this "event," the dog took no further interest in us. He got up and rushed to the wreckage of the demolished cook house to forage for what he could find. It was doubtless the biggest "blow out" he had for many a day.

Some time later, after we entered Germany, I became a hospital case. Before going, I went to Snuffer and told him it was goodbye. I think he understood. He licked my hand and sat back on his haunches and let off the most dismal howl I have ever heard.

Well, that was more than forty years ago, but I can still see every bit of it, every plank and sheet of iron, just as if it had been yesterday. Snuffer was a wonderful dog and one of Nature's gentlemen. If ever a dog deserved a "Doggy Heaven," with a super cook house, he did. I hope he has one!

The Dog Knew

Kate Henning
November 1959

I have read and heard lots of stories about the wonderful instincts of dogs but the experience I had after my sister and her husband, Gertrude and Herman Byerly, were drowned on April 2, 1940, was uncanny.

They owned a large pit bull dog and, while Jack wasn't mean or vicious, he had to know you pretty well before he accepted you. He was patience itself with children, loved to roughhouse with the family, but if he didn't know you—watch out! Bedlam broke loose when anyone came up the back walk or when anyone stepped on the front porch, and, as Gertrude was alone a lot at night, they didn't try to discourage Jack in this.

Gertrude and Herman were drowned around nine o'clock in the morning, but we weren't notified until afternoon. By the time we had attended to necessary details and were ready to go to their house to see about things there, it was late in the evening.

There was quite a group of us, my husband and I, an aunt and uncle, Mr. and Mrs. Roy Marlow, my husband's parents, and several other people. Nevertheless, when we went up on the porch there wasn't a sound from Jack. We assumed the Byerlys had taken Jack with them, although no one had seen him at Boston Lake, near Lewis, Indiana. However, I knew

32

that no one could get into the house without Jack raising a fuss.

Ten or fifteen minutes later I heard a noise from the basement, and I remembered that sometimes Gertrude put Jack in the basement when they were going to be gone a while. Jack and I were good friends so I didn't hesitate to go down to investigate. When I got to the foot of the stairs I didn't see Jack and was about to go back up when I heard him whimper. I followed the sound and found Jack hiding behind the furnace. He came to me willingly enough, but he was shaking as if he was having a chill, as if terribly afraid.

I coaxed him upstairs where he did not bark or show any interest in the other people at all. We thought it strange that this dog no longer protected the house where he had never let anyone, friend or foe, enter without barking and continuing to bark until he was assured it was all right.

He had been devoted to Gertrude and Herman and I believe that Jack, through some extrasensory perception, knew that Gertrude and Herman were gone.

He never was the same afterwards and, although he was only eight years old, he only lived a few more months after his owners' deaths.

Do Animals Have ESP?

D. Scott Rogo
July 1986

Stories of pets and other animals with psychic powers have inspired legends and campfire tales. But many of these stories are true. The story of Bobbie, a collie lost by his owners in Indiana, is told in Charles Alexander's *Bobbie: A Great Collie of Oregon* (1926). Bobbie made headlines when he walked for 3,000 miles back home to Silverton, Oregon; it took him six months. The late J. B. Rhine investigated a 1951 case in which a cat, left behind in California, made its way across country to its owners' new home in Oklahoma.

Stories of dogs that howled piteously when their distant masters were killed also abound in literature. Reports of animals predicting disasters have led to studies of the possible psychic abilities of some animals.

For years parapsychologists in this country and in Europe have been experimenting in the laboratory with canine, feline, and rodent subjects. Their work adds a fascinating chapter to the history of parapsychology.

Probably the basic question concerning animal ESP is whether it is widely distributed throughout the animal kingdom. Just how many kinds of animals possess ESP? If ESP is a natural ability, one would expect all animals—not just highly evolved ones like dogs and cats—to possess a sixth sense.

This hypothesis has led some researchers to experiment with primitive animal forms, to see if they have some extrasensory powers. Parapsychologists in Great Britain, for example, demonstrated back in the 1950s and 1960s that even the tiny paramecia (one-celled animals visible only through a microscope) and wood lice can at least receive ESP messages. The experimenters placed the little critters on glass plates and then "willed" them to swim or crawl up, down, left or right. A different direction was chosen for each trial, of course. This simple experiment was repeated over and over and the animals often moved in the direction toward which they were telepathically commanded. Similar experiments have been conducted with sea worms, caterpillars, and ants.

Even fish seem to possess ESP powers. Dr. Robert Morris, a former colleague of mine at the Psychical Research Foundation in Durham, North Carolina, demonstrated this when he was still working at the Institute for Parapsychology (also located in Durham). (This is the old Duke University Parapsychology Laboratory which moved off campus to become the Foundation for Research on the Nature of Man; the Institute became its research organ).

Morris used a simple T-maze for his experiment. An animal is released at the base of the "T" and will be forced to turn either left or right when it reaches the junction at the cross-area of the stem. Morris filled the T-maze with water, released fish into it and tried to will them to turn either to the left or to the right. His attempts were only marginally significant.

Morris designed a more complicated experiment to test the fish for precognition. This test also was conducted under the auspices of the Institute for Parapsychology. Morris, an animal behaviorist, knew that fish become agitated when facing a threatening situation, so he placed three goldfish in a tank and had an assistant monitor their behavior to determine which fish acted most agitated—which fish swam about most.

After the assistant had made his observations, Morris caught one of the fish in a net and held it aloft over the tank—which should be a highly traumatic experience for a fish! He chose the fish randomly, but found that often the one he caught in his little net was the fish his assistant had designated the most "agitated." He concluded that the fish had actually foreseen this life-threatening experience.

The results of this experiment, however, were still only marginal. Morris decided that the results were not stable, reliable, or replicable.

Very little work was done with animals during the 1950s and '60s. Most parapsychologists felt it was more fruitful to work with people than with fish, dogs, cats, or rodents. The research done with animals was intriguing but did not show strong results. All this was soon to change. The world of animal ESP research (anpsi research, for short) received a boost in 1968 when two French scientists, writing under the pseudonyms of Pierre Duval and Evelyn Montredon, reported their new technique for testing the ESP powers of mice. This experiment was easy to run, harmless to the animals, and, according to the scientists, highly reliable. They conducted their research at the Sorbonne in Paris.

The design of the Duval-Montredon experiment was simple. The scientists used a specially constructed box which was divided in half by a low barrier. A grid capable of conducting an electrical current was placed at the bottom of the cage. The box was then hooked up to a generator which delivered a series of shocks to either side of the cage in random order. A shock was sent every minute or so. Since most animals have a strong aversion to electrical shock, the experimenters wished to determine whether mice placed in the apparatus could determine precognitively which side of the box was about to receive the shock and so jump over the barrier and escape it.

The mice did, of course, jump over the barrier when they received a shock; this was a normal response to the discomfort. But the French researchers noted especially those moments when the mice jumped across the barrier for no apparent reason. These they called "random behavior trials." By testing the mice over and over again, they discovered that the rodents tended to jump over the barrier when the side of the cage in which they had been placed was about to be shocked. This tendency was too consistent to have been the result of coincidence. The mice seemed to know when and where the shock was coming, and jumped the barrier to avoid it.

Duval and Montredon conducted a series of these tests before submitting their research to the *Journal of Parapsychology*, the official publication of the Institute of Parapsychology. The Durham people were excited when they learned of these experiments because it seemed the French researchers had discovered a consistent way of studying ESP in animals.

The task of replicating the French rodent research fell to W. J. Levy, a young doctor who had only recently joined the Institute staff. Dr. Levy reported a series of consistent replications of the French research. In 1974, however, this research was called into question when he was caught faking some of his later research, so it is an open question whether the French work was really confirmed at Rhine's laboratory.

Although fascinated by the original Duval-Montredon work and Levy's alleged replication of it, European researchers were unhappy that the animals were punished by shocks if they didn't show psychic capabilities. Consequently, several of them began designing rodent-ESP tests which rewarded rather than punished the animals if they succeeded. This allowed them to conduct their tests with a clearer conscience.

Some of the first work along these lines was done by Sybo Schouten at the University of Utrecht, which has long maintained an excellent parapsychology laboratory. Schouten planned to see if his mice could use ESP to get nourishment. He began by training the mice in a special cage equipped with a water-feeding tube. A lever inside the cage controlled the feeding system. A light bulb, also located inside, was the key to success. The mice were taught that they could get a drop of water by pulling the lever down, but only when the light bulb flashed on.

After the mice had learned how to work the lever and water system, they were tested for ESP. They were placed in a new box which had two levers. A generator randomly determined that only one of the levers would release water from the tube at any given time. Schouten hoped that each mouse being tested would be able to choose the correct lever, once the light bulb went on. The test was successful since, after a great many trials, Schouten was able to determine that the mice were choosing the correct lever more than the expected fifty percent of the time.

Schouten went on to design what may be called the first experiment in "mouse telepathy." He conducted the same experiment outlined above but with one catch. A second mouse was placed in a separate, but identical box, and was shown which was the correct lever to push. It was Schouten's idea that the second mouse might be able telepathically to inform his little cousin which lever to choose. This experiment was also successful.

Researchers in England also began to test rodents for ESP by using rewards instead of punishments. They too were successful.

Another intriguing development came to parapsychology's attention during this time. The fuss and furor caused by the Duval-Montredon work gradually led some parapsychologists to ask an even more provocative question. If animals can make psychic contact with the outside world through some sort of sixth sense, might they also be capable of controlling it? In other words, do animals possess psychokinesis as well as ESP?

The pioneering work in this controversial area of parapsychology was the brainchild of Helmut Schmidt, a German physicist who first settled in Seattle where he worked with the Boeing Laboratories. Because of his interest in parapsychology, he eventually moved to Durham, where he joined the staff of the Institute for Parapsychology. His first experiments were with very simple forms of life, such as algae, and even yeast cultures. Not until he began working with cockroaches did he hit the jackpot.

Dr. Schmidt conducted his first successful experiment at the Institute in 1970. He placed cockroaches on an electric grid which was hooked to a generator. At regular intervals the generator would activate and either deliver a shock to the grid or withhold it. Shock delivery was entirely random. This meant that when the cockroaches were placed on the grid for a series of trials, the generator would deliver shocks only fifty percent of the times it was activated. Schmidt believed that, if the cockroaches possessed PK ability, they would use their powers to zap the inner workings of the generator and cause it to malfunction so that it would deliver shocks somewhat less than fifty percent of the time.

Schmidt tested several cockroaches before making an amazing discovery. It seemed the cockroaches were causing the generator to deliver more shocks than expected. Apparently the insects were seeking out the shocks as a form of stimulation!

The finding alerted Schmidt to a major problem in all parapsychology research. Since he had run the tests with the cockroaches himself, he might have used his own PK on the generator. Schmidt acknowledged that he didn't like working with cockroaches, so his own aversion might have led him unconsciously to punish the insects by zapping the generator into producing more shocks than it should have.

For his next test, Schmidt used his pet cat, and automated the experiment so that he wouldn't have to monitor it. He placed the cat in a shed behind his home in Durham. It gets pretty cold there at night and the only source of heat in the shed was an electric lamp hooked to a generator which randomly turned it on and off. The lamp was programmed to stay on precisely fifty percent of the time in order to stay warm. Since the test was automated, Schmidt left the shed for the duration of the experiment. By remaining inside his house when the test was being run, the physicist hoped that no PK would escape from his mind to help his pet.

The test results confirmed Schmidt's hypothesis. The cat was able to make the light stay on more than fifty percent of the time. Schmidt never was able to replicate this experiment, however. The temperature in Durham started to warm up, and the cat soon learned to hate the shed. She would run away as soon as anyone tried to get her inside.

Schmidt's PK test with the heat lamp prompted other researchers at the Institute for Parapsychology to design similar experiments. They attempted replication using lizards, chicks, and even unhatched chicken embryos, and reported some success. Although there has been relatively little research conducted to explore the PK powers of animals, most of the work that has been done has followed closely along the lines of Schmidt's original experiment. The only major exception was a clever experiment run a few years ago by William Braud of the Mind Science Foundation in San Antonio, Texas.

Dr. Braud, a soft-spoken young psychologist, spent most of his early career studying the learning capacities of freshwater fish at the University of Houston, before turning to parapsychology. His interest in parapsychology led him to join the staff of the Mind Science Foundation, where he decided to test the possibility that fish possess PK.

He designed a novel test to explore this possibility. First he procured two Siamese fighting fish. These fish are so aggressive that they will attack their own reflections. They were placed in a special tank equipped with a mirror which could be turned either toward or away from the fish. The mirror was then hooked to a generator which produced a high-speed oscillation. As long as the generator was running smoothly, it turned the mirror toward the tank a specific number of times. As soon as the fish saw their reflections, they would become agitated; they would change color, extend their gills, beat their tails and put on quite a show.

Braud theorized that the naturally aggressive fish would use PK to interfere with the oscillations produced by the generator, and cause the mirror to turn toward them more frequently than it would under normal circumstances.

He was right. After several days of testing, Braud discovered that the fighting fish did seem capable of affecting the mirror oscillations. To check his finding, he also tested two other species of aggressive fish, as well as common goldfish, which are rather placid. As he expected, the aggressive fish all affected the generator, while the goldfish did not.

Animal PK, unfortunately, has not been as thoroughly researched as has animal ESP. Consequently it is hard to draw any firm conclusions from the relatively few studies conducted to date. Do these studies really indicate that animals possess psychokinetic abilities? It is practically impossible to tell whether the animals are employing their PK powers, or whether the experimenter is contributing the talent himself.

Although many cases of telepathic dogs have come to parapsychology's attention over the years, there has been relatively little experimental exploration to determine whether dogs generally are psychic. Among the work that has been done were some U.S. Army-sponsored experiments conducted by J. B. Rhine while he was still at Duke University.

In 1952, representatives of the army asked Dr. Rhine if he thought dogs could be trained to locate mines buried in battlefields. This was a serious concern of the military. If dogs did possess such a clairvoyant capability, many lives could be saved. Rhine said he would be willing to experiment and try to find out. The army supplied the funds for the project; its only condition was that the tests must be kept secret.

The tests were conducted in California, along a beach north of San Francisco. Rhine's colleagues buried five small wooden boxes to serve as "dummy" mines along the shoreline for each test. Then a dog trainer, who did not know where the boxes were buried, would lead his dogs along the beach and mark the spots where the dogs indicated a mine was buried. The dogs were trained to sit down when they detected one of the boxes.

Over a three-month period, 203 tests were run. The dogs successfully located the mines a little more than fifty percent of the time. This is above what coincidence could account for; the dogs, however, tended to do best at the beginning of the test and then their accuracy diminished.

The U.S. Army eventually abandoned the test because the results weren't consistent enough and training dogs' ESP seemed impractical. The army's main concern was that the dogs seemed incapable of independently searching out and locating the mines; they had to be led through the mock minefield by a trainer.

Probably the most sophisticated experimental work with canine subjects was conducted by Aristed

Esser, a psychiatrist at Rockland State Hospital in New York. In 1975 he undertook a series of ingenious tests, apparently prompted by rumors that Soviet scientists were testing animals for ESP. One of these rumors alleged that Soviet officials had sent out a submarine carrying baby rabbits, while the mother rabbit was kept at a laboratory on the mainland. The story was that when the baby rabbits were either killed or frightened, the mother became agitated at that very same moment. The truth or falsity of this story has never been determined. Nonetheless, the report gave Dr. Esser the idea for his tests.

Esser's tests were to determine whether dogs could respond telepathically when their masters or canine cousins were threatened in any way. In one initial experiment, he made use of two rooms located at different ends of the hospital in which he worked. Two beagles, trained as hunting dogs, were placed in one of the rooms. This room had an observation window which led to an adjoining area, so the dogs could be watched carefully during the test. The owner of the dogs was escorted to the other chamber, given an air-gun and instructed to "shoot" at colored slides of animals flashed on a wall of the room at random intervals. The experimenters then waited to see how the dogs would react during the "shootings." The dogs barked and whined as soon as the hunter started shooting, even though they could neither see nor hear what was going on in the chamber where he was positioned.

Esser was so pleased with his results that when he reported his experiments in 1967 he said he had "no doubt ... that some dogs, especially those with a close relationship with their owner, have highly developed ESP."

Esser conducted a series of follow-up tests. One of these was designed to see if a boxer would react when its owner was threatened. The dog was placed in a soundproof room and attached to a device that kept a record of its heartbeat. The dog's owner, a young woman who had volunteered to take part in the experiment, was asked to wait in a different room in another part of the hospital. She had no idea that the experiment had already begun, so she was startled when a mysterious man barged into the room and shouted wildly. Of course this was all part of the plan. At the exact time the woman was so badly frightened, her dog's heartbeat suddenly accelerated for no apparent reason. The boxer apparently sensed that its owner was in trouble and became agitated.

The doctor conducted a similar test using two boxers. One was a female, the other her male offspring. Each dog was placed in a separate room. When one of the experimenters threatened the younger dog with a newspaper, the mother dog was seen suddenly to cower in the other room.

I think the experiments we have discussed have been fruitful. Other parapsychologists have their own view about the importance and success of animal ESP research.

Dr. Morris, probably the world's leading authority on animal ESP, has acknowledged that "there is some evidence that psi communication is not restricted to humans," but he refuses to speculate on the meaning of his work. "Before more specific speculation on the evolution of psi and its ecological significance can be seriously considered," he wrote in 1977, "we need more data on more species." He points out that, while it certainly appears animals possess ESP, we still know virtually nothing about the hows, whys, and wherefores of their capacities. We are especially in the dark about the conditions under which animals can be expected to make use of their psychic powers.

John Randall, a biologist who pioneered research on ESP in animals in Great Britain, is much more enthusiastic about the evidence. Nor does he hesitate to speculate about the long-range meaning of this work. He believes ESP may have been a power which significantly guided and shaped the process of evolution itself.

Parapsychologists are not the only scientists intrigued by the new vistas opened up by the discovery of ESP in animals. Many conventional zoologists are excited by the evidence. They speculate that ESP may be an "X" factor which contributes to the hive behavior of communal insects such as ants and bees, helps pigeons home, controls the behavior of migrating birds and assists animals in adapting to their environments.

These ideas are speculative, but they remain scientific possibilities. Only time will tell what role ESP plays in the daily lives of animals, but the evidence that they do possess ESP seems unimpeachable.

The Mourning Dog

Jerry Friedman
January 1975

In 1934, when I was five years old, my grandfather had been sick for two years and now was dying.

"Grandpa's goin'," I would hear my mother say.

"Where?" I'd ask.

"Never mind."

At the time my grandparents, Philip and Clara Friedman, owned a grocery store in Brooklyn, New York. We lived "out on the Island" (in South Ozone Park), and my parents Herman and Sadie Friedman went to the store on weekends to help out.

My grandfather had a dog, a huge black German shepherd, which in those days we called a police dog. His name was King and the first time you saw him you knew why he was named that. He was regal. And he was a one-man dog. My grandfather was the man.

While Grandpa was ill and confined to bed, my grandmother had to take care of him and also run the store, so they lived in a room behind the store. Grandpa's bed was placed at the back of the room against a window looking out on the backyard. Because the room was small and King wasn't, he had to stay in the yard where there was a doghouse Grandpa had built for him.

During this period King stationed himself at the window where he could look in at his master. My father told me later that the expression on King's face was pitiful to see. Somehow the dog knew Grandpa was dying and he expressed his anguish the only way he could, with cries, moans, and whimpers.

We were at the store the day Grandpa died, November 10, 1934, and although it was a cold slushy day I was sent outside to play while the body was being prepared for removal. I could tell that King knew it had happened. He stood up on his hind legs, scratched at the window with his paws, and roared his anger.

My aunt Sylvia Schachter said, "Be sure the door to the yard is kept shut all the time. This is no time to let King inside, especially the way he felt about Pa."

My grandfather was buried the next day in Mount Hebron cemetery in Brooklyn, and after the funeral the family returned to sit in mourning as is customary in the Jewish religion. King was strangely silent whenever my father led the family in prayers, but at their conclusion he would continue his anguished howling.

The afternoon of the third day of mourning was very windy. A side gate was blown open and King escaped from the backyard. I was in front of the store playing in the snow when King came racing out into the street.

"King!" I shouted. "Come back, King!" But he ran down the street and disappeared around the corner. I hurried into the house and told my father, and he and some of the rest of the family immediately started searching the surrounding streets. They didn't find a trace of King.

For my family to leave the mourning and go to look for the dog was sacrilegious, but they had done it instinctively, not thinking at the time that they were breaking the Jewish law. Returning to the back of the store to resume the mourning, my father told one of the neighbors about King and the neighbor said he would organize a search party to look for the dog. Everybody in the neighborhood knew King and many were anxious to help.

"Don't worry," they said, "He'll be found." But four days later when the mourning period had ended King had not been found. The neighbors had given up the search. They said, "If he wasn't found by now, forget it. He doesn't want to be found."

But how could the family forget? King was part of the family. We continued the search and placed an ad in the local newspapers—but no luck. All efforts to find the dog were in vain.

One afternoon about three weeks later while we were having lunch, someone said, "You know, there's one place we haven't looked—the cemetery.

"That's ridiculous. How would King know where to go? He doesn't know where Pa's buried. He was locked up in the backyard when they took Pa away."

"I know all the arguments. And yet, I've read of things like this, strange unexplained things. What will it hurt to go out to the cemetery?"

The family went to the cemetery that afternoon. As they turned onto the road leading to the grave there was nothing in sight and my Aunt Sylvia said, "See? I told you. He couldn't possibly have found his way here. It's impossi—"

She didn't finish the word because by then they had reached the grave and everyone had seen the fresh paw prints in the snow.

My father went to find a cemetery attendant. He asked whether a large black police dog had been seen near Grandpa's grave.

"Seen him? You bet I've seen him. He's been around here for weeks. Every day at that grave, lying across it and crying like he'd lost his best friend. When anyone goes near him he stands up and growls. So we just leave him alone. You know something? You can set your watch by him. Every afternoon at two o'clock he shows up, stays awhile, and then runs off."

At the mention of the time my father gasped—the graveside ceremony the day of the funeral had been at 2:00 P.M.

At 1:30 the next afternoon, December 9, 1934, my father was back at the cemetery, waiting. At two o'clock King had not come. The cemetery attendant saw my father and came over to him.

"Strange, it's after two and he ain't here yet. He's always here. Never misses. This is the first—wait a minute. There he is."

My father looked up. King was standing on a slight rise, looking down at the grave. My father called to him, then ran toward him, but King turned and disappeared over the rise.

He was never seen again.

Animal Ghosts

A considerable body of folklore attests to worldwide beliefs concerning the reality of animal apparitions. But folklore—the belief that something happened somewhere to a usually-unnamed somebody—is one thing; the personal experiences of those who have encountered disembodied beasts are quite another. Anyway, why not animal ghosts? If there can be phantom ships, trains, cars, and houses—all reliably reported, at one time or another—there surely can be phantom dogs and cats. But a ghostly mongoose—that talked?

Ghost Dog of the Kiamichi Mountains

Edouard Jacques
as told to A. L. Lloyd
August 1961

In the early part of 1879, farm work was so scarce in eastern Indian Territory (now Oklahoma), that about March 1st I decided to ride south to the foothills of the Kiamichi Mountains. I had heard a lot of new settlers had come into that area and were leasing land from the Indians.

I rode south for about five days. I had a bedroll tied behind my saddle, but never had occasion to use it for I always managed to arrive at a settler's house by late evening and they always asked me to "get down, tie your horse to the fence (or hitching rail), and come in." They were glad to have visitors, if only to get news from other parts of the country. They never would accept any pay for the night's lodging.

About the middle of the afternoon of my fifth day of riding, I passed a small log house about fifty yards west of the road. I paused for a few moments, but decided it was early yet and rode on.

About half a mile further south, I passed what I took to be an old Indian cemetery, on my right, on a gently sloping hillside. It was overgrown with dead grass, weeds, and bushes. There had been a rail fence around it, but it had rotted and fallen down. Only rough native stones stuck in the ground marked the graves.

After passing the cemetery, about fifty yards south and probably 100 yards from the road on the right, I noticed a small, tumble-down log house. A half-mile farther was a large-size, double log house. From the looks of the house, barn, and fences I knew here was a farmer who took pride in his handiwork and was prospering.

Of course, the dogs announced my arrival. A man of about forty-five years old came to the door and on out to the gate. I introduced myself, told him where I was from, that I was looking for farm work, and asked could he keep me for the night.

"Sure, I can keep you for the night," he said. "Get off your horse! We will take him to the barn, unsaddle, water, and feed him, then we will go to the house and talk while the wife is getting supper."

His name was Matthews. We went onto the porch, where I washed up and then we sat and talked till supper was ready. Like all pioneers, the Matthews were hospitable and friendly, eager for news from other parts of the country.

At the supper table, Matthews and I talked of the new settlers coming in every year, building homes and renting from the Indians, thus benefiting the Indians as well as themselves. He asked, "Do you remember passing a small log house up the road about a mile from here?"

I told him I did.

"Well, that man, Brady, is badly in need of a farm hand. He settled there a year ago last winter. He hired three different men last year, but before a month was out they all called for their pay and left. If you want work, he has plenty to do. You can ride over early tomorrow morning. I'm sure he will hire you. He has no accommodations to lodge a hired hand, so we have arrangements whereby his hired hand can sleep here. We will furnish breakfast. You ride over, do a day's work, he furnishes dinner and supper, and then you ride back here for the night. He pays the hand $15.00 per month and pays me $5.00 per month for your sleeping and your breakfast here."

I told him that was all right with me.

After an early breakfast, I rode over to Brady's. A woman, who appeared to be in her middle twenties, came to the door. I introduced myself, told her I had stayed at Matthews' place last night, that he had sent me over as I was looking for farm work.

"Yes, we need help and if you will follow that road," she pointed to the right and west of the house, "you will come to the field where Mr. Brady is plowing."

I followed the new-made road for 250 yards, came to a pole and brush fence, and saw Brady coming back from the far side of the field, following a plow and team.

I repeated my story and he asked, "Can you go to work after noon?"

I said, "I can go to work as soon as I can change to my work clothes."

He told me to take the plow and team while he did some more clearing and building fence. At noon I heard someone tooting a cow horn, Brady appeared out of the brush and said, "Dinner time."

Brady, I knew, was pleased with my handling of the team and plow, and at dinner his wife also seemed pleased. She remarked, "We've had so many hired hands, but they don't stay long."

I told them I would stay as long as there was work to do.

At sunset the horn tooted again. I unhitched, drove the team to the house and by the time I had taken care of the horses for the night, supper was ready.

When I started back to Matthews' it was dark, but a beautiful star-lit sky made it light enough to distinguish and identify objects. I had a summer's job that would extend into late fall. I rather liked those evening rides and an hour and a half's talk with Mr. and Mrs. Matthews before bedtime. The job became routine. I rode over in the early morning and back again at night.

I had been at work about two weeks when one evening just after dark, as I approached the old cemetery, I noticed a small white object moving down from the cemetery toward the road. As it neared the old rotted-down fence, I could make out that it was a black and white fox terrier. As I passed, it leaped and landed on the horse behind me. I always carried a quirt on my saddle horn, but never had to use it on the horse. I jerked it off the horn and whipped around behind me two or three times before I realized I was hitting nothing. Looking over my shoulder I could still see the dog riding behind me. I reached around with my hand to pull the dog off but, like the whip, my hand went through thin air without touching anything. Still I could see the dog perched behind me. I put my horse to a gallop, thinking I would throw the dog off, but he stuck with me until I got about even with the tumble-down cabin. Then he disappeared.

This was on Friday night. I said nothing to the Matthews about my experience, but I had noticed that whenever I came in they glanced at me quizzically, as though they expected me to tell them something.

I soon learned that "Foxy" would ride with me about twice a week, generally on Tuesday and Friday nights. I found myself watching for him, hoping he would ride with me. We became pals.

I had been there nearly four months when, one Saturday evening, Brady had me quit work early because Mr. Matthews had invited us all to have supper with them.

After supper, we sat out on the front porch and talked on every subject imaginable, until the conversation led up to ghosts. Brady asked me right out if a black and white fox dog had ever ridden with me.

"Oh, yes," I replied, "Foxy and I are good pals."

Brady looked at me in astonishment. "Do you mean to say that he rides with you twice a week and you never try to avoid him?"

"No," I answered. "After that first night, when I found that he was a ghost dog, I had no fear. Although I've often wondered about the cause of his appearing."

At this Brady said, "Mr. Matthews, tell Edward [he could not exactly pronounce the French name Edouard] the story of Foxy. I never expect to get another hand that will stay as you have. Foxy was the cause of my other hired hands leaving."

Mr. Matthews began his story of Foxy:

"About three years ago, in April I think it was, about 4:00 in the afternoon, I was reading in the living room, when the dogs announced someone was coming. I walked out on the porch and saw a man riding toward the house. About the first thing I noticed was a black and white fox terrier riding behind him on a mat or pad.

"He rode up to the gate and asked if I could lodge him for the night. I told him we could and invited him to get off his horse and come up on the porch. Foxy jumped down and immediately made friends with our dogs.

"He introduced himself as Jacobs, said he was a Civil War veteran, had been wounded in the chest and, as the wound seemed never to heal, the doctors advised a change of climate. He had read a great deal about Indian Territory and the Kiamichi Mountains, so he thought he would try this climate for a year. He talked with a slight foreign accent, said he was German. He received a small pension from the government.

"The next morning Jacobs said he wanted to ride around and look the country over. He left his bedroll on the porch and said he would be back in the afternoon, that if we could lodge him for two or three days, he would pay. After he got on his horse he just said, 'All right, Foxy.' The little dog leaped onto the horse behind Jacobs.

"As you know, Ed, there's a pile of rotting logs at the southwest corner of the cemetery. When Jake came it was an abandoned shack in fairly good condition. Jake asked if I cared if he fixed it up and lived in it. I told him to go ahead, even helped him chink up the cracks, patch the roof, and build a cot against a wall. We fixed him up with some cooking vessels and Jake was at home.

"He would ride down to the village once a week, buy a few groceries and seemed to get along fine. He rode all over this country and learned it better than I.

The summer passed, and as fall approached we began to get cool nights.

"About four o'clock one afternoon in early November, I noticed a deeper blue in the northwest. The air became chilly, and in thirty minutes it had clouded over and one of those dreaded 'Blue Blizzards' was upon us. It began to rain a cold icy rain.

"Jake didn't get in until nearly dark and he was soaked to the skin. He had had no coat, as the day had started out warm. He asked to stay in the house that night and also asked me to bring his clothes from the shack. By this time he was getting so hoarse he could scarcely speak above a whisper.

"After I got him into some dry clothes, and built a fire in the east room, I told my wife to look after him while I went for the doctor at the village, three miles south. By the time Doc and I got back to the house Jake had begun to choke up and had difficulty breathing. After a brief examination, the doctor said a case of double pneumonia was developing rapidly. Although Doc did all he could Jake gradually grew worse. By morning Doc said there were no hopes of him pulling through. Doc stayed all day, but by two o'clock that afternoon Jake had sunk into a coma. Foxy knew there was something wrong with his master. He sat outside the door, on the porch, and howled. We finally let him in and he ran straight to the bed, jumped up by Jake's side and licked his hands and face. We fixed him a pad at Jake's feet and he lay there with his jaw resting on his forepaws, watching Jake's face.

"At five o'clock Jake took a turn for the worse. Doc said he was dying. Foxy seemed to think so, too. He crawled up to Jake's face, licked it, and made low, piteous moaning sounds. About six o'clock Jake breathed his last. At the same time, Foxy jumped off the bed, ran to the door to be let out, just as though he knew his master was gone and wanted to go with him. I watched him and he headed straight to the old shack. I could hear him crying and howling.

"Doc drove my team and buggy to the village and sent a couple of fellows back with it to sit up with the dead during the night. Four or five men came out early next morning to dig a grave. Foxy came to the house when the men drove up. We let him in and he went to where Jake was laid out. I uncovered Jake's face. Foxy licked it once, then went out on the porch and cried.

"By three o'clock the grave and coffin were finished and we laid Jake to rest. Foxy lay at the head of the grave watching the men work. As we left the cemetery, Foxy still lay there grazing at the fresh mound. I tried to coax him to the house but he refused to come along.

"About ten o'clock that night I went out there and Foxy was lying where we had left him. I took something for him to eat, some water, and the pad he rode on.

"Next morning I went out to the cemetery and Foxy was lying where I had seen him the night before, his food untouched. I carried him to the house, let him in the room where Jake had died. He walked all around the room sniffing and whimpering, reared up on the side of the bed once, then wanted out.

"As cold weather was coming on I built a shelter over and around Foxy. I knew he would never stay at the house. Besides, he wouldn't eat and drank but little, if any, water. Two weeks later I went on my regular morning trip to the cemetery and found Foxy dead.

"That dog died of grief. I dug a deep hole by the side of Jake's grave and buried him.

"Nearly three months after Jake's death, a lone horseman passing the old cemetery about dark saw a black and white fox terrier coming down from the old graveyard. The dog mounted behind the rider, who almost ran his horse to death getting away from there.

"People for miles around here know about Foxy's ghost. But you, Ed, are the first man to ride with Foxy for a summer and say nothing about it."

I never got back down there after that summer. I have often wished I could go, just to see the changes that have taken place since statehood, and I have wondered if Foxy still rides behind some lonesome horseman on Tuesday or Friday nights.

Little Boy on a Ghost Horse

Bob Lee Austin
April 1960

In the year 1904, on a farm near Alderson, West Virginia, it was about eight o'clock in the evening and Mrs. Fay Baker sat in her rocking chair on the front porch enjoying the fresh, cool breeze after a hot, strenuous day of farm work.

The night was peaceful. The stars were bright in the sky. The moon hung in the firmament like a huge disk of burning gold. There was something strange about the moon tonight, and the stars, too, and even about the night itself, Mrs. Baker thought as she sat and rocked.

Mr. Baker was out at the barn doing his evening chores. The five Baker children were in bed, tired after working all day.

Suddenly Mrs. Baker heard the hoofbeats of a galloping horse. Then, in the field across from the house, she saw her son Ralph, age seven, astride a beautiful white stallion. Ralph was laughing. He was laughing louder than his mother had ever heard him laugh before; but it didn't sound like a happy laugh. It sounded weird.

Mrs. Baker was startled and surprised, to say the least, for she had thought Ralph was in bed, but the great white stallion occupied her attention. She was obsessed with its beauty. In all her life Mrs. Baker had never seen such a beautiful horse, and her son was riding it like a professional horseman!

She watched hypnotically as the horse galloped swiftly past the house, carrying her hysterical son on its strong back.

"Ralph! Whose horse have you got?" Mrs. Baker called. "And what are you doing out of bed? Don't you know you've got to work tomorrow? Ralph, do you hear me?"

But the horse and rider were out of earshot.

Mrs. Baker watched as her son turned the stallion around about a half-mile from the house and headed it back toward her.

The magnificent horse approached rapidly. What a beauty!

Ralph's laughter filled the semi-darkness of early night with an eerie ring as the space between him and his mother grew shorter.

"Ralph! Whose horse is that?" Mrs. Baker called. "You hear me, Ralph? Stop that silly laughing so you can hear me."

But Ralph didn't stop laughing.

The stallion shot past the house.

Mrs. Baker watched until the horse and rider dropped out of sight behind a hill. Then fear gripped her. She stood transfixed on the front porch, unable to move. Once again the night was silent—so silent she could hear her own heart beating.

Suddenly Mr. Baker came round the corner of the house, frightening his wife even more than she already was frightened.

"What in the world are you screaming about, Fay?" he demanded. "I thought something was wrong with you."

"Ralph!" she answered, pointing toward the hill behind which her son and the white stallion had disappeared. "Ralph! He just rode away on a horse—on a big white stallion."

Mr. Baker merely stared at her unbelieving.

"Well don't just stand there!" she snapped. "Go and find him. That horse'll throw him yet. Go on, get a hurry on."

"But Ralph's in bed. He went to bed before I went to the barn."

"Well he's not now. He just rode a horse past here not more than three minutes ago."

Mr. Baker began to believe his wife. "I'll get the lantern," he said, and went into the house, his wife right behind him.

They went through the living room and into the bedroom where the boys were sleeping. It was dark in the room, but not too dark for Mr. Baker to count three small forms in their beds, the three small forms of his three sons. Ralph was lying on the outside.

Mrs. Baker counted them too. "I ... don't un-understand," she stuttered. "I saw him just as plain as day—riding a big white stallion. And he was laughing crazier than I've ever heard him laugh before." Mrs. Baker went over to the bed.

It was Ralph, all right. He was there.

Mrs. Baker put her hand on his forehead and quickly jerked it away. Ralph's skin was warm but clammy, like that of a person who has just died.

"Fred!" she screamed. "Something's wrong with Ralph! I—I think he's dead."

Mr. Baker rushed to his wife's side. He felt his son's wrist. There was no pulse.

Ralph Baker was dead, and hadn't been dead more than eight minutes.

At that moment, that precise moment, hoofbeats were heard outside the house, and laughter louder than Mr. and Mrs. Baker had ever heard before filled the night.

The Bakers ran out on the porch.

That magnificent white stallion was prancing around in the field across from the house; and on its back sat Ralph Baker, laughing like an imp.

Mr. and Mrs. Baker were gripped with fear. They couldn't believe their eyes. Yet they both saw and heard the same thing, the great white stallion, with their dead son on its back, laughing a laugh that wasn't of this world.

Then the stallion reared on its hind legs; Ralph held onto its mane and together they shot away into the darkness.

Ralph Baker had ridden out of this world on a ghost horse.

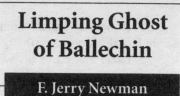

Limping Ghost of Ballechin

F. Jerry Newman
December 1952

In 1892, John, third Marquess of Bute, a member of the Society for Psychical Research, met a Jesuit priest from whom he heard a strange account of an allegedly haunted house in Scotland.

The priest, Father Hayden, S.J., confided that he had slept only one night out of the nine he had spent as a visitor in Ballechin House, Perthshire, being disturbed by queer, inexplicable noises every night except the last.

He added that, of all the strange manifestations during his stay, the sound that alarmed him most was that resembling a large animal throwing itself against his bedroom door.

In August, 1896, Ballechin House was rented for a period of twelve months to a wealthy Spanish family. They left suddenly after a stay of only seven weeks, forfeiting more than ten months' rent rather than stay longer in the house.

In 1897, Lord Bute, together with a Colonel Taylor, Miss Goodrich-Freer, and other members of the S.P.R., rented Ballechin House for the purpose of conducting a thorough investigation of the phenomena.

Guests who had stayed at Ballechin testified that they had been disturbed by groans, rappings, and other violent and unexplained noises. Often they were awakened by sounds of dragging footsteps, which traversed the passages and circled their beds. Sometimes, in the middle of the night, an unearthly shriek would ring through the house.

Ballechin House was owned by a Major Stewart who retired from military service in 1850, some sixteen years after succeeding to the property. He was passionately fond of dogs and he kept fourteen of them. A lifelong student of psychic matters, he was convinced that the spirits of the dead were able to return to earthly friends and surroundings.

A deep interest in werewolves and vampirism led him to assert that, far from being empty superstition as was popularly believed, lycanthropy (the changing of a man into an animal) was a fact. He affirmed on many occasions his intention of returning after death in the form of his favorite spaniel.

The Major died in 1876, and so powerful had been his influence that, immediately after his death, all his dogs, including his favorite black spaniel, were shot. Shortly afterward, phenomena of an unusual, often violent nature broke out.

The whole household would be roused by the manifestations, and on one occasion five male guests, dressed only in their night shirts, met at the top of the stairs. They were armed with sticks and pokers, and one of them carried a revolver.

Heavy footsteps and the pattering feet of invisible dogs were heard in empty rooms. Groans accompanied heavy knocking. Spectral figures were seen and on several occasions the colonel was awakened during the night by the bed clothes being lifted mysteriously from his bed.

A butler, Harold Sanders, who had been with the Spanish family that fled from Ballechin so abruptly, wrote a letter which was printed in *The Times* during the Ballechin House controversy, which occupied the columns of that paper from June 8 to 24, 1897. Mr. Sanders wrote:

"I kept watch altogether about twelve times, in various parts of the house. When watching, I always experienced a peculiar sensation a few minutes before hearing any noise. I can only describe it as like suddenly entering an ice house and feeling that someone was present and about to speak to me ..."

Of one experience he wrote: "I shall not forget it as long as I live. I had not been in bed three minutes before ... my bedclothes were lifted up, first at the foot of my bed, but gradually coming towards my head. I held the clothes around my neck with my hands but they were gently lifted in spite of my efforts to hold them. I then reached around with my hand but could feel nothing.

"I could distinctly feel and hear something breathing over me. I then tried to reach some matches that were on a chair by my bedside, but my hand was held back as if by some invisible power. Then the thing seemed to retire to the foot of my bed. I suddenly found the foot of my bed lifted up and carried around towards the window for about three or four feet, then replaced to its former position."

These extracts from a rather lengthy letter serve to confirm what at first appeared no more than speculation—that the phenomena were directed with greater intensity against permanent residents than against visitors. The staff at Ballechin were continually dogged by noises and apparitions.

One of the maids, Elizabeth, slept in a room by herself, while two others slept in an adjoining room. One night, Elizabeth woke to see, hovering above her bed, a mist-like cloud, which changed shape continuously as she watched. As it sank lower, she felt her bedclothes tugged.

Presently, the coverlets were lifted clear of the bed. The maid was so frightened that she lay for a long while unable to move or utter a word. When she recovered, her screams were so frightening that the other maids were too scared to go to her room. From that time on, the three girls slept in one room.

It was about this time that the "dog" phenomena reached their peak. Visitors who brought their own animals with them to Ballechin remarked on their strange behavior. Two guests saw their dogs romping with another dog, a black spaniel, which vanished as strangely as it had appeared.

A lady guest was awakened one night by the whining of her dog, which was lying at the foot of her bed. She saw two black paws resting on a table at her bedside. No other portion of the strange dog was visible.

Another lady, like many others, had been repeatedly disturbed by the sounds of limping footsteps which circled her bed. Shortly afterward, she heard stories about the former owner. She asked if he could be described.

"Well," said her informant, "the most striking thing I can remember about him is that he had a peculiar limp." And he gave an exhibition which tallied exactly with the limp she had heard around her bed.

During the investigation conducted by Miss Goodrich-Freer and Lord Bute, Miss Freer kept a journal in which she entered the details of all phenomena. Under the date February 16, 1897, she wrote:

"About 10 A.M., I was writing in the library and presently felt a distinct, but gentle, push against my chair. I thought it was my dog (Miss Freer owned a black Pomeranian) and looked down, but he was not there. I went on writing, and in a few moments felt another push, firm and decided, against my chair. I looked backward with an exclamation—the room was empty."

February 21: "Heard noise of patterings ... Scamp (Miss Freer's dog) got up and sat, apparently watching something invisible to us, turning his head slowly as if following movements across the room. The interest which our dogs took in these phenomena led us to the conclusion that the sounds were those of a dog gamboling."

Remarkable as were these phenomena, there were others during Colonel Taylor's tenancy which were witnessed by numerous members of the household. These included the apparition of a woman in grey, a spectral nun, the bent, white-haired figure of a limping man, and a phantom crucifix which appeared momentarily to one of the guests, and which was seen again, some time later, held by a materialized hand.

But through all these manifestations the dominant phenomena appeared to focus around the limping footsteps and the phantom dogs, sometimes incredibly reinforced by the familiar doggy smell so common during the days of the Major.

On many occasions, visitors and servants heard the quarreling voices of a man and woman, their tones loud and rough, their words indistinguishable. It seemed a repetition of the scene of the Major brow-beating his housekeeper as he did in life.

For more than a decade, dour parishioners and voluble village tradesmen gossiped about the "queer goings on up at the House." The Major's idiosyncrasies appeared as lively a source of interest after his death as they had been during his life.

Incredible, perhaps. But all the evidence points to the fact that the Major kept his promise and on more than one occasion he returned—either with or as a dog!

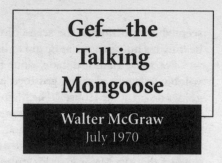

Gef—the Talking Mongoose

Walter McGraw
July 1970

Once upon a time, on a tiny little island, in a tiny little house, there lived a tiny little animal named Gef, who made wee-wee on a great big psychical investigator and screamed: "Go away, clear to hell! We don't want you here."

Not true, you think? Let me warn you that, in the 1930s, one R. S. Lambert, then of the British Broadcasting Company, investigated Gef and said, "It is impossible to deny that there is serious evidence ... for Gef's reality ..." And Lambert was called "crazy," but after lengthy proceedings, a British court awarded him 7,000 pounds damages; in effect acknowledging there indeed was good reason to believe in the existence of a talking mongoose on the Isle of Man.

Man, with its 50,000 people spread over 227 square miles, lies northwest of England. It is said that on one of its few clear days you can see England, Scotland, Ireland, and Wales from the top of Man's highest peak, Mt. Snaefell. Its principal source of income is inexpensive tourism. For a short time in the summer months the island is inundated with holiday visitors from what Manxmen call "the adjacent island"—England. The rest of the year, Man is a fairly lonely place to live, especially if you happen to be on one of the rocky little farms that dot the countryside. To one of these farms at Doarlish Cashen, owned by James T. Irving, a 58-year old former traveling piano salesman, Gef came in 1931.

In his own way Irving was as much an anachronism as Gef. He was well-educated, always neatly dressed and a farmer whose hands remained clean and uncalloused. Mrs. Irving, four years younger, bore some resemblance to England's Queen Mary, and Viorrey, their 12-year-old daughter, was a quiet, serious child, given to wandering alone on the moors. It was said that she could sneak up behind a rabbit and kill it with a club, while her dog Mona held the rabbit's attention by mesmerism. Never off the island, nor, for that matter, even visiting the northern half of the small Isle, she must have been a curious mixture: part wild lonely child of the moor, part developing young lady, old beyond her years and filled with a wonder imparted by her much traveled, story-telling father.

The farmhouse itself was small, two-storied and cheerless, its solid stone walls broken only by a few cramped windows. Inside, for insulation, the walls had been lined with dark matchwood paneling which stood off a few inches from the cold stone. This characteristic of the house created a condition which made possible the story of Gef. It seems Gef liked to live in a house where he could not be seen and yet could satisfy his gregarious nature. The space between the stone and the paneling pleased him immensely, as did the ceilinged stairway. The wonderful resting place above that ceiling Gef called his "sanctum."

Gef probably lived in the house for some time before he made himself known to the Irvings—which he did by knocking on the walls and making a variety of animal sounds. Then once when Irving asked his wife, "What in the name of God can he be?" the animal spoke.

"What in the name of God can he be?" echoed from the walls in a voice pitched two octaves above a normal woman's.

From then on the animal quickly learned to speak not only English, but to use the many foreign phrases the widely traveled Jim Irving used—as did Viorrey, following her father's example. But in the beginning there was no closeness between the strange animal and the Irvings. He liked to throw things, and since his sanctum was in Viorrey's room, the thought of injury to the child bothered Irving—and thus he discovered the little animal's greatest weakness. He tried to kill the animal—first with poison and then with a gun. This brought immediate reaction in the form of damage to the house and profane screams so threatening the Irvings moved Viorrey into their room for fear she would be killed. It seemed nothing affected the little beast as much as a threat to his own life.

It took six months to bring about a truce. By that time the family had begun to like Gef, as he called himself, and he promised to protect, not hurt, Viorrey. Mrs. Irving began to leave bits of food for him in the sanctum. These he ate and shared with Viorrey, whom he often followed into the fields where he jealously threw stones at anyone who talked to her. (His aim was said to be very good.) Then, too, he began to pay his own way by strangling hundreds of rabbits, which he left for the Irvings either to eat or sell at seven pence each. "The God-damned mice," as he called them, he frightened by meowing like a cat. But it was a long time before any of the family actually saw their boarder.

"You'll put me in a bottle if you catch me," he often said, and he gave other reasons for not letting anyone see him, saying he was a freak, a ghost, and part of the fifth dimension, but it all boiled down to his fear of being caught and killed. When visitors came he often would disappear, returning only after they left. Then, emitting gales of screeching laughter, he would tell of his adventures on other parts of the island.

Gef was an incurable gossip and the Manx population became wary of Irving because—mysteriously to them—he knew so many things he should not have known. They began to dislike the little spy even more when he took to stealing, carrying his loot home as presents for the Irvings. When he began stealing sandwiches at the bus depot and cadging rides underneath some of the buses, a bus company mechanic rigged a trap to electrocute him. Irving learned of this and warned Gef.

Gef, for once, was not afraid. He said the trap was attached to Bus No. 82. Irving checked and found Gef was correct.

Around the farm, Gef was always active. He threw stones at unwanted visitors, urinated through cracks in the wall, killed more rabbits, and learned to amuse those few visitors he liked by peering through a hole in the ceiling and calling a tossed coin—"heads" or "tails"—when none of the Irvings was in the room. Other times he mischievously locked Viorrey in her bedroom with a lock that could not be reached from inside her room. He also would throw heavy furniture, no mean trick for an animal estimated to weigh only a pound and a half.

As time went on Gef began to show himself to the Irvings—but infrequently. They saw him walking the rafters. Viorrey hid outdoors once and saw him. Mrs. Irving put her finger into a crack in the wall and felt inside his mouth and was bitten for her pains. Gef apologized for drawing blood and killed a rabbit to make up for it. Finally he even let himself be photographed, but he was so nervous that Viorrey, not very experienced with a camera, never got a satisfactory portrait.

Those who saw Gef said he had a bushy tail like a squirrel's, yellow to brownish fur, small ears, and a pushed-in face. His most-often described features were his front paws, which, according to Irving, were hand-like, with three fingers and a thumb. Gef claimed to be an 83-year-old mongoose, and said he had come from India many years before—but he fitted the description of a mongoose about as well as he did that of "part of the fifth dimension."

Irving suggested he might be a cross between a native rodent and one of several mongoose that actually had been brought from India to the Isle of Man some years before. If so, he was indeed a freak. No known mammal in the world, according to naturalist Ivan T. Sanderson, has three fingers and a thumb. Over and above that, however, Sanderson points out that a mongoose could not crossbreed with a rodent.

Of course, investigators came from England to look into this story. A reporter from the *Manchester Daily Dispatch* heard Gef speak. The reporter was with Viorrey at the time. Capt. M. H. MacDonald, businessman and racing driver, paid three visits to the farm at Doarlish Cashen. He heard Gef speak, both inside the house and out, had stones thrown at him, and witnessed the coin-calling trick. Once he and Irving walked four miles to Peel for lunch, had some beer, talked about Mrs. Irving's shoes, and picked a wildflower. When they returned to the farm, Mrs. Irving met them outside the door and recounted their doings. Gef had followed them and reported home before their arrival.

Harry Price, director of the National Laboratory of Psychical Research, and Lambert, (whose damage suit was mentioned earlier) went together to Man to investigate the story, but Gef was afraid "the spook-chaser" would trap him and put him in a bottle. Psychiatrist (then psychic investigator) Nandor Fodor did not meet Gef, but talked to many persons who had.

For a while, the story of Gef was a world wonder. There was even an offer of $50,000 for a six-month tour of the United States. Gef turned this down, screaming, "They would put me in a bottle!" Finally, when Gef, who never had been seen by any of the investigators, refused to talk or play his tricks when strangers of any kind were on the premises, interest waned. Except for mentions in a few books touching on poltergeists, Gef was forgotten.

In 1946, the little animal came briefly into the news again when Leslie Graham claimed to have killed him. Graham had bought the Irving farm, and said that several times in the fifteen months of his tenancy he had seen a large black and white, weasel-like animal disturbing his chickens. He had set snares from which the animal always escaped. Finally, hearing a great disturbance in the farmyard one October morning, he found the animal snarling in the snare. He then had taken a club and killed the beast.

He described the animal as about three feet long, weighing five pounds, one ounce. He skinned it, and its pelt was "as thick as cow skin, indicating that the animal was very old."

This seems an inordinately sad ending to one of the most charming tales in all paranormal literature. One could only take hope from the disparity between Graham's description of the animal he killed, and the Irving's description of Gef. On the other hand, could Gef have grown that much bigger in a decade? A final consolation: if death had come to him at ninety-five, as computed from his own claims, his worst fear at least was not realized. He was not put in a bottle.

Did Gef ever really exist? And if so, what was he?

Many writers and a few persons I talked to on the Isle of Man find it easy to dismiss the entire episode as a hoax, considering Viorrey the principal culprit, of course. They accuse her of being a ventriloquist who began playing tricks which were built to unbelievable proportions, first by her father, and then by newspaper reporters looking for copy where little could be found. One early investigator, J. Radcliffe of the *Isle of Man Examiner,* said he caught Viorrey squeaking once when he was with Irving. Irving, however, insisted the noise came from another part of the room.

Most of the investigators who actually went to Doarlish Cashen saw enough to convince them that Gef was more than the product of the Irvings' imaginations. They base this conclusion on the facts that Viorrey could not have been a good enough ventriloquist to have fooled them all; that doors could not have been locked from the outside by any of the family; that much of Irving's knowledge about other parts of the island could be explained only by granting the existence of Gef; and that the Irvings would not have kept up such a hoax for so many years for no profit. Also they point to the killed rabbits and the stones thrown against the outside of the house when all the family was inside.

Early on, psychic investigators postulated that Gef was a poltergeist or even a ghost. Manx people (the few who will talk about Gef at all today) speak of him as "the spook." But Fodor, both in his book *Haunted People,* co-authored with Hereward Carrington (E. P. Dutton & Co., 1951), and in conversation, argued against both of these explanations.

True, as in classic poltergeist manifestations, Gef showed up at about the time Viorrey was going into puberty—but he did not go away until at least 1938. This does not follow the classic pattern at all. Moreover, Fodor pointed out that a poltergeist never is seen at all and does only harm. Gef threw stones and spit on people during his fits of temper, but he also furnished meat in the form of rabbits, and did such errands as going downstairs to look at the clock when Irving asked him to. As for the ghost explanation, how often has a ghost been known to eat biscuits and chocolates, and then urinate?

Which brings us to the final possibility. As Fodor wrote in 1937, "Is Gef an animal that talks? All probabilities are against it, but all the evidence is for it."

Fodor, a twentieth-century psychiatrist, believed in "possession." He postulated that Irving, a man much reduced in circumstances, "obsessed" some small animal and molded it to his own personality. The shock of being a life-long failure split off part of Irving's personality, which contrived the animal in order to fill his time, build his ego—in other words feed "the mental starvation" from which he suffered in the wilderness of the Isle. Fodor pointed out many similarities between Gef's personality and Irving's. Both were dictatorial when crossed, and both were overly possessive of Viorrey. Finally, the little animal served to bring outsiders to Doarlish Cashen and to attract attention to a man who could not have been satisfied with the intellectual caliber of his farm neighbors.

I think it was in my last conversation with Fodor that the subject of Gef came up again. While in *Haunted People* he sounds a bit tentative in his suggestion, over the years he seemed to have become surer of his hypothesis. However, he had lost track of the Irvings by that time and wondered if Gef had gone with them when they left the island. Might Gef still be alive somewhere?

As I've said, today Gef is not a favorite subject of conversation on the Isle of Man, but those few who do not speak of him as a hoax seem sincere in their belief that Gef indeed did live. All who knew them regarded the Irvings as honest, respectable people. Also, some people have pointed out that Mrs. Irving seldom mentioned Gef, but when she did she made clear he was an animal, not a "ghost" or "spirit."

Ironically, not on the Isle of Man but in England, some of the answers Fodor wanted came to light when I talked to Viorrey, the last of the Irving household. She is an attractive woman and a knowledgeable conversationalist, but she did not answer the question I most wanted answered. What happened to Gef?

Viorrey says she does not know. The last she remembers his being around the farm was in 1938 or 1939. He seemed to go away for longer and longer periods of time, and then he just never showed up again. He had made no statements about leaving; there had been no good-byes; he simply was gone. No, Gef did not leave the island—with the Irvings, at any rate. Viorrey is certain, however, that the beast Graham clubbed to death was not Gef.

In the animal's gradual leave-taking, Fodor might have found support for his theory about Irving and Gef. Was it merely coincidence that Gef, who always claimed to hate publicity, ceased to be around when interest in him fell off, and no more interesting people came around to talk to Irving about the phenomenon? Perhaps Fodor would say that Gef no longer served Irving's purpose.

Fodor also would have been interested in the denouement of the story of Gef. Today, more than thirty years later, Viorrey hates Gef. In the early days, she and Gef were inseparable, playing games and sharing sweets, but as she grew older, Gef seemed closer to her father. Fodor noticed in 1937, and reported at that time that Gef seemed to have outstripped Viorrey in mental growth. He wrote, "The grasp and thirst for knowledge of the Talking Mongoose is simply phenomenal ..."

And what of Viorrey in 1937? No longer a child of the moors, she had become a young woman who wanted a social life and friends, and more than anything else she wanted to be accepted. By that time Gef had become a burden.

"I was shy ... I still am," she said. "He made me meet people I didn't want to meet. Then they said I was 'mental' or a ventriloquist. Believe me, if I was that good I would jolly well be making money from it now!"

I cannot divulge where Viorrey lives now or the type of work she does, but she is not rich. The only money the Irvings ever made from Gef, besides the sale of rabbits, was five pounds Fodor paid for his week's room and board, and an occasional guinea paid for newspaper pictures. According to Viorrey, Gef cost them dearly. They had to sell the farm at a low price because Manxmen called it "haunted."

"Gef was very detrimental to my life. We were snubbed. The other children used to call me 'the spook.' We had to leave the Isle of Man, and I hope that no one where I work now ever knows the story. Gef has even kept me from getting married. How could I ever tell a man's family about what happened?"

Was Gef a mongoose?

"I don't know. I know he was a small animal about nine inches to a foot long. I know he talked to us from the wainscoting. His voice was very high-pitched. He swore a lot."

The speech was not parrot-like?

"Oh, no. At first he talked to me more than anyone. We carried on regular conversations."

After thirty years you still insist this was not a hoax?

"It was not a hoax, and I wish it had never happened. If my mother and I had had our way we never would have told anybody about it, but Father was sort of wrapped up in it. It was such a wonderful phenomenon that he just had to tell people about it."

Fodor regretted that the mystery of the talking mongoose probably never would be solved. He felt that "the power which he (Gef) displayed must have had a human origin." He believed that clues obtained from studying that "power" might have given us leads about many strange and still mysterious aspects of the human personality and possibly explain poltergeist phenomena (though he did not believe Gef was pure poltergeist).

I can make no claim to having brought us any closer to a solution, but after talking to Viorrey, the last principal involved (assuming Gef died or perhaps just faded away), two things fascinated me.

First, is Fodor's hypothesis correct? If we could talk about it together today, I would be less skeptical.

Second, I spent an entire day with Viorrey, talking of many things. She knows of the British newspapers' propensity for paying high prices for "expose" stories. Yet, despite her position on the financial ladder, she will not even talk to reporters who have tried to trace her down, presumably with offers of money.

Someday I may have to eat these words, but I found myself believing this woman when, with every emotional and financial motive for saying otherwise, she said very simply, "Yes, there was a little animal who talked and did all those other things. He said he was a mongoose and said we should call him Gef ... but I do wish he had let us alone."

Animal Magic

Animals, real, paranormal, or imaginary, are used as instruments of magic, often for malevolent ends.

Phantom Wolf

J. P. J. Chapman
September 1956

Even now, the West Country of England is host to superstition, witchcraft, magic, and strange happenings of all kinds. Most of the villages have their own grey lady, headless horse, and local witch.

The village of Parcham where I lived was no exception, and often, as a boy, I listened with popping eyes to stories of the phantom wolf. These stories told how, on certain nights, the wolf howled around the village and could be seen loping in the moonlight along the Green Walk which led from my home to a gardener's cottage at the edge of the wood.

One of the older men of the village, a jovial fellow named Tapp, assured me that in his father's day the wolf had been shot in the leg and the next day old Amy Prouse, a witch who had lived in the next village, was seen to be limping. When questioned about her bandaged leg, she said she had cut it while chopping wood!

Tapp also said that, as a small girl, Amy had been seen collecting certain herbs from the hedges. When asked why, she had replied, "I'm picking victuals for mother's toads."

Her mother had been the wise woman of the nearby village of Aston. Tapp had gone to see her about his warts, and she certainly knew how to get rid of them—

with the orange-colored juice of an herb which grows freely in Somerset. He had found her cottage a fascinating place. Bunches of dried herbs hung from the old oak beams. Dried toads, pots of powdered snake skin, and bags of charred feathers lay on shelves. On the mantel over the wide, open hearth stood many curious clay figures. Hanging within the chimney itself, so wide that one could peer up and see the sky, was an assortment of dried animal hearts stuck with pins. The local chimney sweep vouched for the truth of this also, as these mysteries were taken down and carefully placed aside when he swept the chimney.

Love charms and ceremonies were part of the old lady's strange trade. One such ceremony included piercing the dry shoulder blade of a rabbit with a needle. It was to be pierced nine times and each time the following jingle was recited:

> This bone I do not mean to prick
> but through my true love's heart I mean to stick
> and may he neither rest nor sleep
> until he comes to me and speaks.

The bone was then burned in the fire, and results eagerly anticipated.

Beauty treatments were part of her stock-in-trade, and truly she and her daughter, Amy, had marvelous complexions that with the years did not turn sere and yellow and were remarkably free of wrinkles. To this day, there is a recipe for one of her beauty masks used in the village.

Through the years I questioned many people in the village, and it seemed that Amy Prouse and the phantom wolf were, in some way, connected. Tapp was convinced that she had been able to turn herself into a wolf when it suited her. Of course, she had been dead for many years now and why she should walk as a wolf was a mystery, but, according to many people, walk she did, and always as a wolf. Those who saw this wolf swore that it was so powerful it even could cross water by walking on the surface.

I was told that the wolf loped across many miles of country, through valleys and glens, from the village of Aston, where Amy Prouse had lived, to the Green Walk near my home. I was particularly fond of this part of the garden. During good summer weather, my friend Tom Turner and I often camped out there. It was a delightful spot—a wide, grass-grown walk between overhanging oak trees, and not in the least bit eerie. At the end of the walk stood an old, thatched, white-washed cottage with a tangled, overgrown garden. It had not been occupied for many years, for the village people swore that the water in the nearby well was bad. The old wellhead was overgrown with brambles, and the gear above it had long since disappeared.

The last gardener to live in this cottage had been Ted Prouse, a distant cousin of Amy's. He had been a queer, miserly chap who lived alone with only his old collie dog, Nelly, for company. Nelly had disappeared mysteriously one evening. She was never found, and a few weeks later Ted had died.

Tapp told me that Amy had come over from Ashton to clear up the cottage and take away the few bits of furniture. He remembered his father saying that she had made a great fuss at finding no money in the house, and was worried because she could not find a three-handled quart cup that had belonged to her mother.

I was having a drink with Tapp one evening in the summer of 1912 and, as usual, reminiscing over Amy and her witchcraft, when I decided it might be a good idea to camp out in the Green Walk that night. The weather was fair, although with a slight tendency to thunder, and, *who knows,* I thought, *I might see the phantom wolf.* Finishing my beer, I dashed off to see Tom Turner. He was quite pleased at the idea of sleeping under canvas for a few nights, and together we collected our camping equipment, eventually settling down comfortably for the night with one side of the tent open. However, I could not sleep. It was very warm and close. Occasional flashes of lightning were visible in the distance. Silvery green and black patterns danced on the grass. Nearby an owl hooted mournfully.

Lying on my side and looking through the open tent flap, I suddenly became aware of something moving along the Green Walk. My skin grew taut and a prickly feeling ran over my scalp. Thinking I must be dreaming, I turned to look at Tom. He was awake also.

"Look, Tom," I gasped. "Look, along the path. Isn't that the phantom wolf?"

Tom laughed and said, "Good Lord! Surely you don't believe that nonsense," but as he looked in the direction in which I was pointing, his eyes widened in fear. There, advancing slowly toward us and outlined in a luminous glow, was a huge wolf. Its jaws seemed to salivate with a phosphorescent drip. As it approached, an evil smell filled the air. I began to recite the Lord's Prayer aloud. Tom hurriedly joined me. As we reached "deliver us from evil," there was a blinding flash of lightning, followed by a rumble of thunder. At the same time the wolf suddenly changed his course and made off along the walk toward the cottage. As we watched, another form emerged from the brambles near the wellhead. It appeared to be a grisly, greyish old collie dog. There began a soundless but truly horrible fight between wolf and dog. Over the well, around the well, they snarled, rolled and jumped. Eventually the wolf seemed to lift the dog into the air and it disappeared into the well.

Horror-struck, we watched as the wolf, still out-lined in a greenish glow, loped off toward the cottage, and entered it through the closed door.

Another flash of lightning released us from our stunned, immobile state. We realized that the cottage had been struck and already was blazing freely. The thatched roof and old timbers were very dry. Hurriedly pulling on our trousers, we dashed off for help, but in those days there was not even a telephone in the village. By the time the local fire brigade arrived, the cottage had burned to the ground.

Some years later, another cottage was built near the site of the old one. The well was cleared out and rebuilt. During this renovation, a curious three-han-dled quart cup, nearly filled with coins, was found in a niche in the side of the old well, and the skeleton of what appeared to be a collie dog was taken from the bottom of the well.

I have never found the courage to sleep again on the Green Walk—to find out if the wolf still runs there.

The Devil Snakes of Ansuam

Lloyd A. Smith
April 1959

"White man know plenty of things," said my African cook one day, "but many things he do not know. The jungle—it hides magic no white man can understand. Only ju-ju men understand it."

I got the idea he was frightened of something and when I grinned at him reassuringly he shook his head. "White man has no understanding of terrible things black man's magic can do," he growled.

It was in the Ansuam jungle that I saw and felt African black magic at work. Unlike the African cook who tried to warn me, I am still no believer in ju-ju, witchcraft, fetish, or any other superstitions of the Gold Coast natives, but I admit that I can't explain the strange series of events which began in 1939 when, as an underground surveyor at the Touan Gold mines, forty-five miles inland from Takorandi on the Gold Coast, I was sent out to survey a route and peg the site for a pipeline to bring water from a dam in the jungle-covered hills.

In two weeks, the bush-clearing men, Fantis and Wangaras, hacking away with axe and machete, had cleared four miles. Then suddenly the bush thinned and the work grew easier.

We were near the small Fanti bush village of Ansuam, on rising ground, when suddenly I heard the native men shouting in anger. I found two of them arguing with a repulsive old Fanti, a character who was completely naked, covered with ashes, and who had a bunch of stones dangling from the lobe of each ear, which had been stretched by this treatment until they were nine inches long. He was crawling with flies.

Yelling abuse at the men and waving a yellow stick at them, he was saying that the little valley was no good for strangers, especially white men; that we had better get out and stay out, or else.

The men seemed frightened and sheepish, but they pushed past him. About 200 yards further on, we came to the explanation. A ju-ju house stood there, a small but sturdily-made shelter of mud and thatch, with the bush tramped down for about ten yards all around it. The skulls of dogs and oxen formed a circle on the ground. The hut was covered with red clay decorations, and weird designs in black and white pebbles studded the walls. It lay squarely on the line of the pipe, so it had to come down. Drinking water for the native workers was, in the company's opinion, more important than preserving a witch doctor's mud hut. I could imagine the face of my Chief Engineer if I put a kink in the pipeline merely to appease native superstition.

I told the crew to demolish the hut, that the witch doctor would be paid compensation many times its worth as a shelter. To my astonishment, they refused. With hangdog expressions and drooping shoulders they slunk to one side, muttering that the hut was the lair of a powerful ju-ju which could do us great harm.

Refusing to waste any more time arguing, I took a crowbar from a Fanti and smashed a hole through the mud wall of the fetish hut. An unearthly howl went up from the witch doctor who had followed us. The Fantis, shrieking with fear, ran off into the bush as though 10,000 devils were pursuing them.

With the old witch doctor watching me and muttering all the time, I pushed down the walls and dragged the debris to one side so that the bed could be prepared for the pipeline. When the dust had cleared, I found, on what had been the floor of the hut, a heap of rubbish, including two human skulls, some dried lizards, and the decomposed bodies of sacrificial fowls.

Of the men, only Tom, who was a Krepi, had remained. The Fantis did not return until I had finished the demolition, and when they did, they were shaking like leaves and refused to come near the site of the hut. I hacked out the bed across the site myself; then awe-struck, apprehensive, and whispering, the men moved up the line into the virgin bush again. They avoided me, regarding me as a doomed man.

The lead man, Ajiny, spoke to me gravely, "Boss, lookum ground proper," he said. "Then ju-ju get devil. All same Hausa call 'Michiji.' Suppose Boss, no lookout, he die some time."

He was telling me that the spirit of the fetish lived in the body of a snake, and the snake was very angry.

An hour later, we ran into some big trees festooned with creepers. When we cut through the trunk of a huge cottonwood, six Fantis climbed up to hack at the stiff vines that still held it upright. For half an hour it hung fast. Then Tom, the Krepi, passed under the hanging mass. Almost as though by design, the heavy tangle of creeper and branches tore itself clear and fell on the screaming native.

By the time we hacked our way through to him, he was unconscious, with his right leg broken, one shoulder dislocated, and his neck horribly twisted. To the Fantis the situation was crystal clear. Tom had helped me to destroy the ju-ju; Tom was a Krepi and an outcast.

We started to carry him back to the mine hospital. The men gave a wide berth to the site of the ju-ju hut, but I went straight to the tumbled ruin. My curiosity got the better of me and I stopped to examine the debris inside. Among the dried grass something moved, and as I lifted the grass with a survey peg, a living band of scaly green slid swiftly toward my wrist.

Before the thing could strike, I flicked it up with the peg and hit it in the air. Maimed, it attacked three times, and then I caught it a resounding whack six inches behind the head, breaking its neck. The evil, slithering thing was paralyzed, but the head and neck still writhed and twisted, the forked tongue flickering in jaws that were wide open and still ready to deal out lingering, agonizing death.

A snake was only a snake. I had seen and killed hundreds during my years in India and Africa— but this one was different. It was dull green, about three feet long, and on its flat head were two distinct horns, covered with skin and scales, rising about two inches from the skull. The African horned viper! It was the first I had ever seen. I opened my clasp knife and cut off its head, carrying it to my bungalow in a cigarette tin. When the wise old cook saw it, he blanched with terror. His eyes opened as though stilts had been forced between them, and he shivered like jelly.

Evil, he whispered, would follow my feet.

"What sort of evil?" I asked.

He shuffled and gasped for breath, and then explained that his particular ju-ju had personal guardians—horned vipers who follow anyone forever to avenge the destruction of the ju-ju. "Debble snakes," he called them. "Boss," he pleaded, "make you go home, quick, or Boss die."

I had heard superstitious nonsense like this many times before, and the old cook's distress only interested me. After a drink or two, I went to bed, thinking no more of ju-ju, horned vipers, and destruction. But two hours later, I was surprised to find myself wide awake. Something or someone was moving about inside the bungalow. I dressed quietly and went to sit on a deck-chair on the verandah.

It seemed only a few minutes before I heard stamping feet and saw my watchman pounding at something that writhed under repeated blows from his club. When the panting Hausa stopped his pounding and his cursing, the writhing thing lay dead.

It was a horned viper—the second one I had seen in my life, and this one within a few hours of the first!

The watchman said he had seen it cross an open space in the moonlight and stealthily approach the bungalow.

I admit that I began to feel uneasy then, but soon my work in the bush was finished, and three months later I was on a ship, the *SS Anglo-Saxon*, bound for the United States. On the third day out, a fellow passenger, Captain Edwards, told me he was a zoologist and was bringing home three cases of reptiles. They were in zinc-lined cases in the hold, but he was worried about them. He had heard that one deadly snake was missing.

"A horned viper?" I asked.

His jaw dropped as he looked at me. "How on earth did you guess that?" he asked. "The horned viper is one of the rarest snakes in the world and most people have never heard of it. Yes, this is a horned viper, but maybe it didn't get on board after all. Or it may have escaped while we were still in the dock, and wriggled through a porthole."

In the smoking room later I told him the story of the ju-ju. We laughed together over the childishness of it all.

"If that darned snake can pick me out of 200 passengers," I said, "then I might begin to believe there's something in it. But, meanwhile, I'll just forget it."

On the fifth morning I was taking a shower when something slid down the hot water pipes against the bulkhead, struck the edge of the bath, and fell into it. There was no mistaking that ugly, writhing body, and for a moment all my cynical amusement about ju-ju and witch doctors left me. I stood paralyzed, gazing at that ugly, writhing snake wriggling toward me with death inside its lethal fangs.

Then suddenly I reacted. With one hand I grabbed the soft broom the steward had left standing upright at the head of the bath, and with the other I turned the hot water full on. I skipped out of that bath fast, but the horned viper couldn't stop itself in its lunge forward, and caught the full blast of the scalding hot water on its head. It recoiled as though it had been thrown back by some invisible force, and the next moment I held the broom head pinning its neck with its coils encircling the handle. I dragged it along the bottom of the bath and held it, writhing, under the stream of scalding water, at the same time shouting for the steward at the top of my voice. He glanced round the door, saw what was happening, then dashed back with a long-handled axe. With one blow he cut off the snake's head.

Shivering as violently as the old African cook who had warned me about this, I dressed and went to locate Captain Edwards.

"The snake must have been attracted to your state-room by the warmth of the water pipes," he said.

But why the water pipes in my state room? Why not one of the hundred or so other state rooms? Why not the engine room and boilers, where there are miles of hot water pipes?

I have seen only these three horned vipers in my life. Since 1939, I've been back to Nigeria within fifty miles of the village of Ansuam, where these snakes are known to exist, but apparently they haven't heard of the Ansuam ju-ju, for to date I'm still alive.

I Saw the Spirit of All Animal Life

Tom Rousseau
September 1961

Eagle Creek is a small stretch of water, forty-seven miles north of Cody, Wyoming, that flows into the north fork of the Shoshone River in the Absorkie Range of the Rocky Mountains. This creek is missed by most tourists and travelers alike, although it is located only three miles north of Holm Lodge, and seven miles south of Pahaska Tepee, Buffalo Bill's famous hunting lodge in the Rockies.

The incident described here occurred during the time that old Plentyclothes was Chief of the Crow Indians. He always came to Cody for the annual Fourth of July celebration, which was called Wolfe Ville. That was the night for the wolf to howl. The town was turned wide open and the local constable always retired early this particular night.

I was a youngster at this time, which was in July, about 1923, but old enough to drive my father's model-T Ford. The Chief liked me because I would on occasion filch a little of my father's bourbon and give it to him. With a bit of the fire water he would want to go places, and on this particular night he wanted to go hunting.

We started driving up the North Fork and kept on until we arrived at Eagle Creek. We parked the Ford, got out, and started walking, he with a 30-30 and me with a .22 rifle.

As we approached the mouth of the creek, there was a blinding flash of light. We couldn't tell the origin of it, but we both could see in the glare an enormous silver-tip grizzly. His size was absolutely beyond comprehending. The Chief silently motioned to me, and we both sat down. The bear reared up on his hind legs and reached into a pine to leave his claw marks. Then, in just a few moments, he faded completely and, as he disappeared, the light went out. After a time, we lit our flashlights and went over to where the monster had stood. Old Chief Plentyclothes was very brave, but chills were running up and down my spine.

There were no signs of tracks on the ground, but the marks were definitely on the tree.

The Chief then told me I had just seen the spirit of all animal life. He said only a chosen few ever would witness a like spectacle. We drove back to Cody and the Chief left for the reservation the next day.

I told my father, who was the game warden, of my experience on the previous night, and he said, "Son, have you by any chance been sneaking a drink of fire-water?"

A week later we both went up to Eagle Creek. I showed him the tree with the claw marks. It really scared him because from the tip of the marks to the base of the tree it measured fourteen feet.

Animal Omens

According to longstanding traditional lore, animals are able to sense when a human being is about to die. In the stories that follow, the "animals" are not always of the flesh-and-blood variety.

Banshee

Louise Hart
October 1983

We would never know where he came from. Nor would we ever know where he went. All we know is that the dog appeared on June 8, 1975, at my parent's home in South Lawrence, Massachusetts.

He was a purebred German shepherd. He was clean and well-groomed, but wore no collar, license, or tags to tell us that he belonged to anyone or indeed ever had.

My two young sons, Erik and Garett, were playing in their grandparents' yard, when suddenly they found the dog running with them, joining in their fun.

No one had seen him come into the yard. No one cared; although he was a large dog, he was unusually gentle with children. We assumed he must have been raised around them.

We thought he must be a runaway or stray, for his ribs protruded through his coat and he was exceptionally thirsty.

We fed him some scraps and gave him water, expecting him to continue on his way. Stray dogs seldom stay long enough to finish their meals and are almost never around for a second.

But this dog settled in. He played fetch and other games with my sons all afternoon and seemed to be growing attached to them.

At five o'clock we had to leave. The children hoped their new pet would come with them. He was such a beautiful dog that I had become instantly fond of him. My parents, Ernest and Louise Hart, didn't want him and obviously he had no other home. I agreed with Erik and Garett that he needed a good home and was more than willing to have him come with us.

Erik and Garett kissed their grandparents goodbye and called the dog to follow them. He obeyed them as he had all afternoon. He trailed behind us as we went down the walkway. One of the boys ran ahead to open the back door of the car.

But when the dog reached the end of the walkway, he froze, almost as if a wall prevented him from moving farther.

The boys tried to coax him. He wouldn't move. They ran back up the walkway toward the house. He followed. They ordered him to sit, stand, and lie down on command. He dutifully obeyed.

Again and again they went to the end of the walkway. They even tried going through hedges at the edge of my parents' front lawn. Each time the dog refused to move beyond the property line. He would not cross the sidewalk to the car or, for that matter, leave the yard.

The children were frustrated and upset. They thought that the dog had come to play with them and that he was their friend; yet he wouldn't leave my parents' property. He wouldn't even allow himself to be picked up and carried to the car.

My parents were dismayed. They hadn't considered having a dog.

Even worse, the dog favored my father who had never been known for any special affection for animals. Yet somehow my father appeared not to mind this one.

After half an hour we finally gave up trying to take the dog home. It seemed such a shame, since we all assumed that this meant the dog would be gone by morning. At my home he would have had open woods and quiet instead of the noise and confinement of the city.

My parents and I had to promise the children that they could visit the dog after school the next day. But even as we made the promise, my parents and I swapped looks that said we knew that tomorrow we'd be trying to console the children and to explain to them that the dog was a wanderer who didn't want a permanent home.

Nonetheless, when the boys and I arrived the next day, we found the dog and my father sitting together on the front porch.

My father chatted about the dog as if he had owned him all his life. It was a great dog, he said. Not only was he well-mannered and well-trained, he was also companionable.

My mother couldn't believe how attached my father was to the German shepherd. My father, who had never owned a pet in his life, seemed to enjoy this one fully. Maybe with the way the neighborhood was changing, with break-ins and gangs of young people on drugs, the dog was just what they needed, my mother decided.

It made sense—not that they had any real choice, since the dog still refused to cross the boundary of their property.

The dog played with the children in the afternoon, but stayed again at my father's side when it was time for us to go.

My children accepted the dog's desire to live at their grandparents' home. They were thrilled that he seemed to love their grandfather so much. They were convinced that his attachment to their grandfather showed that King (we had named him after a dog I had owned as a child and to whom he bore a remarkable resemblance) was the wisest and smartest of dogs. Grandpa was worth that much love.

I took my children to visit their grandparents and King the next two days. And then it happened.

The call came early Thursday morning. My father had suffered a heart attack and was in the hospital. I was frightened and concerned. Mother and I had worried much about him, about the possibility of his having a heart attack, about his failing health. Now our fears had become reality.

Over the next several days, running back and forth to my parents' house and the hospital, I didn't think much about the dog. I was glad he was there for my mother and she seemed comforted by his presence, but it was hard to remember that he was around. He stayed in the spot near the front porch where my father had always come to sit and talk to him. As if sensing what was happening, he stayed as quiet as possible—until the fourth day.

Even as I drove up to the front of the house, I could hear him as he lay by the porch, half crying, half moaning.

I checked to see if he had been hurt. He hadn't. He had food and water but wouldn't touch either. He just lay there making what quickly became an unnerving sound.

My mother, badly frightened, declared it was an omen. I disagreed. The news was all good on Dad. He was recovering and his doctors were saying he'd be home in three weeks.

But that Father's Day was the last time my mother and I were to see my father alive. His heart gave out that evening. The suddenness of his death had a devastating effect on us all.

Mechanically we fed the dog, whose howling had never stopped. We were trying to prepare for the funeral and had little time to comfort the animal.

Concerned about the effect of the howling on my mother's nerves, I ordered the dog to be quiet once or twice, but my mother admonished me. Somehow she felt solace in the unearthly wailing of the dog.

King was still crying the morning we left the house for the funeral. We had given him fresh food and water, but he hadn't eaten since my father died.

After the services, when we returned to the house, all was silent. The dog was gone.

None of the neighbors had seen him leave. The children and I looked for him but to no avail.

I was annoyed. My mother needed the companionship, protection, and comfort the dog could provide—but he was nowhere to be found.

I talked of widening the search for the dog, to look for him in other neighborhoods, on other streets. A dog that size couldn't just disappear.

"You won't find him," my mother said.

"Why not?" I asked. "He's a big dog. Someone must have seen him."

"No," my mother insisted, "you don't understand. He was a banshee."

"What's a banshee?" I asked in tone that betrayed what I was thinking: grief had caused my mother to take leave of her senses.

"It's a spirit that comes to warn a family of an impending death," she said. "In Ireland it's said to be a woman who wails. My grandmother told me she had once heard one. I am convinced that the dog was one. You heard its wail. It knew that your father was passing before we did—and it's gone now. Its mission is done. No one saw it come. No one saw it leave. You won't find it." She shook her head.

My children and I searched the neighborhood for days but found no one who had even seen the dog. My mother was right. King had vanished as if he had never been.

The Raven-Haunted Hapsburgs

Pauline Saltzman
July 1955

A blue haze gently embraced the mountainous terrain between Munich and Ischl, and to all appearances the carriage heading toward Ischl carried a congenial family to one of the many summer resorts nestling in the fir-clad mountains. Actually, Archduchess Ludovica, sister of King Ludwig I of Bavaria, and aunt to His Imperial Majesty, Franz Josef I, was taking her daughter, Helene, to the castle where the girl's betrothal to her young Imperial cousin was to take place. Helene was not enthusiastic. This was just another instance where a royal union between cousins—the mothers were sisters—was being forged in the interests of Hapsburg policy. Everything was arranged—with one exception. No one had reckoned with Elizabeth, Helene's sixteen-year-old sister, also in the Wittelsbach entourage.

Sisi, as Elizabeth was lovingly called by her family, seemed still a child, a vibrantly beautiful tomboy, whose great loves were horses, dogs, and the scenic splendor of her native Possenhoffen. The fairy-tale charm of the region where she was born seemed to have imparted to her the whimsicality and charm that were so uniquely her own.

As soon as the Bavarian archducal family arrived at Ischl, the marriage arrangements were started. But it was too late. Franz glimpsed his young cousin, Sisi, and fell madly in love with her. For the first time in his completely dominated life he refused to obey his mother, Archduchess Sophia, who had engineered his marriage with Helene just as she had connived the abdication of his senile old uncle, Ferdinand.

Franz and Sisi were married April 24, 1854, at Saint Augustine's in Vienna. Overnight this radiant young girl became Empress of Austria and consort of His Apostolic Majesty, King of Hungary, Bohemia, Croatia, Slavonia, Galicia, Lodomeria, Illyria, and Jerusalem. In his early twenties, Franz Josef could boast more titles than any other contemporary monarch in Christiandom.

The Imperial pair was deeply in love, but the marriage was doomed. Sophia could not or would not forget that her desires had been ignored. She made life miserable for Sisi. Sisi's babies were taken from her at birth, so that they might be "suitably reared." Sophia even resorted to throwing exotic court women in Franz Josef's path to distract him from his young wife ... and what Hapsburg ever resisted feminine charm?

In her unhappiness and frustration, Elizabeth paid little heed to the whisperings among the ladies and gentlemen of the palace, who spoke in hushed tones of seeing the "White Lady" of the Hapsburgs, traditional harbinger of evil. Nor did the girl pay attention to reports that the Hapsburg *Turnfalken*, which also presaged tragedy for the Imperial Family, were currently seen and heard. These were the same birds that had wheeled over the ancient fortress of Olmutz when gentle, senile Ferdinand relinquished the Dual Crown in favor of his young nephew. The evil ravens were seen, too, at every Austrian defeat on the battlefield.

The desperately lonely Empress had no one to whom she could turn. With all her honest heart, she detested the empty pomp of the Hapsburg Court. Perhaps the first person to understand her was Marguerite Cunliffe-Owen, to whom Elizabeth became greatly attached and who occupied a prominent place in her suite. Marguerite was to achieve world-wide recognition as the anonymous author of two biographical works on Franz and Elizabeth respectively, *A Keystone of Empire* and *The Martyrdom of an Empress.*

Marguerite herself had a strange and frightening experience which would one day bear tragic fruit. She and the Empress had been spending a few weeks on the Breton coast, but Elizabeth was recalled to Vienna. Marguerite decided to finish her holiday.

One cold November afternoon as Marguerite rode her favorite horse over the wild Quiberon heath in the vicinity known as La Mer Sauvage, she suddenly saw a white figure outlined against the sunset, swaying to and fro on the edge of a rocky precipice. She checked her mount so violently that the sensitive animal reared in the air. It took several minutes to soothe his feelings, though her own were far from calm, but when he was quiet, she forced herself to look back. The figure had vanished. Terror-stricken at the thought of the "White Lady" and what her appearance portended, Marguerite headed back for the castle.

Because of a ball held that evening at the chateau, Marguerite retired later than usual. She was awakened suddenly in the middle of the night, she thought at first by the little rococo bedside clock which was chiming the time. She was trying to go back to sleep when she heard a slight rustle, followed by soft, swift footsteps. In the moonbeams which filtered through the window, Marguerite distinctly saw the same figure she had perceived that afternoon on the edge of the precipice. There could be no mistake; it was Empress Elizabeth! Marguerite was wild with fear as the phantom sadly pointed to her breast where two or three drops of blood slowly oozed from a small, triangular wound.

Marguerite did not give herself the opportunity to determine the nature of her nightmare. She immediately telegraphed the Empress, who promptly replied that she was enjoying the best of health. When the friends were reunited in Vienna, Marguerite was careful not to mention the shockingly prophetic incident.

Elizabeth and Franz Josef never were able to mend the rift in their marriage. Franz was kind, considerate, and notoriously unfaithful. Elizabeth, humiliated but proud, drove herself relentlessly about Europe. Wherever her restlessness drove her, she was shadowed by the dual curse of the "White Lady" and the black birds of the Hapsburgs. People attached to her suite saw them. Elizabeth herself believed in their existence.

On the night of January 30, 1889, the ominous Turnfalken were seen and heard as they flew out of the blood-red sunset, screaming as they wheeled to the south, precisely in the direction of Mayerling Forest where Crown Prince Rudolph, Elizabeth's only son, was keeping his final tryst with his commoner sweetheart, Countess Marie Vetsera, in a hunting lodge. That same night, the "White Lady" appeared, according to official record. In a matter of hours, the world heard the shocking news that the married Rudolph and his mistress were the victims of a murder-suicide pact.

Elizabeth drove herself about Europe more mercilessly than ever after this scandalous death of her beloved son. On the night of April 24, 1898, the date marking her wedding anniversary, a singular scene took place in the corridors of the ancient Hofburg Palace in Vienna. The halls were silent, except for the muffled steps of the sentries as they made their rounds. Occasionally the intense stillness was punctuated by the sharp rattle of musketry from the ramparts. Now and then a guard's challenge rang out, disrupting the silence.

In one of the Hofburg corridors, at a little past midnight, a sentry saw a feminine figure clad in filmy white, carrying a lighted taper, approach him. A stolid Styrian peasant, the guard promptly challenged the stranger, who certainly had no business in the silent corridors of the ancient palace which adjoins the Augustinian church where Elizabeth and Franz Josef were married. The lady in white, on being challenged, turned and retraced her gliding steps. The curious sentinel followed her down the dark passage until he saw her enter the chapel. He alerted the other guards and a thorough search of the premises was made. It was no use. The mysterious lady in white had disappeared.

The guard apparently did not know of the Hapsburg legends. When he and his brother-guards discussed the matter, he heard about a "White Lady," and learned for the first time that such an apparition always warned of impending doom. The Styrian guard's experience became a matter of official record and then the sentries stationed at Schonbrunn, the Imperial summer palace, began to speak of a similar occurrence. The

"White Lady" had been seen there the same night, one hour later!

In the summer of 1898, five months later, the Empress was visiting the Grand Hotel at Caux, Switzerland. One Friday morning in broad daylight, as she relaxed on the balcony, her attention was attracted by a lady dressed in white, who stood before the building. She stared at Elizabeth in so evil a manner that the Empress called an attendant. The grounds were searched thoroughly, but the lady had disappeared. The bushes were beaten and every tree trunk explored, but no one was found.

That same evening, Elizabeth again sat on the balcony when a lady in white—no one knows if it was the same woman—appeared and settled herself under one of the umbrella tents. The Empress at first ignored her but, as in the morning, the hostile stare became unnerving. The ensuing search by the attendants Elizabeth called was diligent and thorough, but again the white-clad lady had disappeared.

A few days later, September 9, 1898, Elizabeth strolled at Territet with her English reader, Mr. Barker, who thoughtfully brought along a basket of luscious fruit. They seated themselves upon some mossy rocks overlooking the magnificent Alpine scenery, and Mr. Barker began to read from *Corleone* by Francis Marion Crawford. By some strange coincidence, this novel dealt with the activities of the Mafia, a secret society which specialized in the assassination of royal figures. Elizabeth, who always traveled incognito, constantly was exposed to this ever-lurking danger, but she cared little. Unknown, even to her, she was shadowed assiduously, not only by the crack Austrian Imperial Police, but also by the famous M. Paoli of the French Suruette, whose business it was to protect royalty from assassins.

Just as she was about to hand Mr. Barker a half of a peach, a huge raven suddenly flew down from the branches of a pine tree. It encircled the air over the Empress' head with the tip of its black wing, knocking the fruit out of her hand. Barker was speechless with terror, for he knew only too well that the sign boded no good.

About noon the next day, at Geneva—five months after the appearances of the "White Lady" at Schonbrunn and the Hofburg Palace—the Empress, accompanied by her lady-in-waiting, Countess Sztaray, left the hotel to board a steamer which would take them to Mont de Caux. They were walking in the direction of the Quai du Montblanc when the Countess heard the clanging of the ship's bell, which she realized was the signal for departure. She walked rapidly ahead, signaling frantically to the crew of the *Geneva* not to remove the gangplank and leave them behind.

During that split-second of time, Luigi Luccheni, an Italian anarchist, who had managed to elude the surveillance of the Swiss authorities, leaped from his hiding place and pounced upon the Empress, driving a shoemaker's awl into her heart. He ran for his life, but was soon overtaken. It happened so suddenly that not even the victim realized what had happened. Passers-by rushed to Elizabeth's aid and she got up dazedly, murmuring something about having been attacked by a pickpocket. It wasn't until she had gotten on board the *Geneva* that she fainted. Upon examination it was discovered that the awl, sharpened to a deadly point, had formed a tiny triangular wound from which oozed a few drops of blood. The weapon had closed the wound, and the Empress, now unconscious, was dying of internal hemorrhage. The steamer put back to shore and a litter was improvised with oars and a sail. But the doctors could do nothing. Elizabeth's wound was exactly the same as the one Marguerite Cunliffe-Owen had beheld on the phantom of the living Empress a few years back! The "White Lady" and the Turnfalken had told their story truly!

For nearly a thousand years the "White Lady" and black birds heralded tragedy for members of the Austrian Imperial Family. They continued their hauntings, although never appearing simultaneously, until the dissolution of the Austro-Hungarian Empire in 1918.

The origin of the "White Lady" is shrouded in mystery. It is possible, of course, that she is the same "White Lady" who has haunted the German ruling house of Hohenzollern also.

When Maria Theresa, first wife of the Emperor Francis, was a girl in Naples, an old seeress predicted that she would marry a widower and die at age thirty-four. The first half of the prophecy came true and the family lived in mortal dread of the second. When the ominous shadow of Napoleon loomed over Europe, she became very ill and her life was despaired of, especially since she had to be moved from the fortress of Olmutz as the foe approached, but Maria Theresa survived and her health improved so remarkably that by the end of December she joined Francis at Holitsch. Her thirty-fourth birthday came and went without a cloud to mar the occasion.

In March of the same year the Emperor began his campaign in Hungary, leaving Maria Theresa, who was expecting their eleventh child, behind. On the night of

April 5, 1807, the "White Lady" appeared at Schon-brunn Palace. There were several eyewitnesses, including the Empress and her young daughter, Marie-Louise. The Empress became seriously ill the following day and died three days after the birth of her little daughter. Eight days transpired between the appearance of the "White Lady" and Maria Theresa's death!

Marie-Louise saw the family ghost on several occasions, for the first time when she was a precocious child of five. Countess Wrbna, her governess, described the "White Lady" as looking like "a court lady, who never did anything to anyone." She simply glided by in her snowy robes and veil, looking majestic and lovely, but she appeared only to warn and to prepare. Her visits were rare, although the Emperor Francis saw her twice in rapid succession prior to the death of his first wife, the Archduchess Elizabeth, and before the death of his father, Emperor Josef, who died the very next day.

The legend of the ravens' origin comes to us from Marguerite Cunliffe-Owen, who tells us that in the eleventh century, near the region where the Aar and Rhine rivers join, there lived a great noble, Count von Altenbourg, also known as Guntran-le-Riche. One day, while hunting in his forest domains, he was attacked by a flock of vultures that would have killed him had it not been for some onrushing ravens who defended him. From then on Altenbourg protected the ravens to whom he felt he owed his life. He built a watch tower on a rock-like promontory, naming it Habichtsburg (Vulture Mountain), from which comes the name, Hapsburg, sometimes spelled Habsburg. Gontran, who was actually the founder of the Imperial Family, provided the birds with food and shelter. The ravens prospered and increased, building their strong nests throughout Gontran's lands.

A century after Gontran's death, the Archabbot Werner and his brother, Radbot, became owners of the lonely watch tower. They added to it until the majestic Schloss Hapsburg proudly reared its battlements and turrets above the giant forests. The birds protested in their own way against the desecration of their retreat. They became so violent that the Hapsburgs began killing them. They were exterminated finally, two centuries later. In the centuries that followed, the birds, or their ghosts, foretold death and destruction to the Hapsburg family.

They were seen hovering over the head of Queen Marie-Antoinette of France, a Hapsburg by birth, when she was taken to the guillotine. Marie-Louise, who had seen the "White Lady" at Schonbrunn, saw the birds during her sad journey from Austria to marry Napoleon, whose own career ended ignominiously. They also were observed, following closely an appearance of the "White Lady," just before Elizabeth's sister, the Duchess d'Alençon, was burned to death in the horrible fire that broke out at a Paris charity bazaar.

Archduke Albrecht, uncle of Franz Josef, had a lovely young daughter who was burned to death at Schonbrunn, immediately after appearances of the "White Lady" and the Turnfalken; though the appearances were not concurrent.

When Archduchess Charlotte and her husband, Maximilian, who was Franz's younger brother, were taking their last stroll before embarking for Mexico where they were to rule under Imperial auspices and against the wishes of the Mexican people, they, too, saw one of the black Turnfalken. It alighted on a bench and landed deliberately upon the Archduchess' train. In 1867, immediately following the documented reappearance of the "White Lady" at Schonbrunn, Maximillian's life was taken by a firing squad at Queretaro. Charlotte lost her sanity after heart-breaking and futile efforts to rescue her husband.

One of the Turnfalken's most significant appearances was in 1894, when Franz Josef's young nephew, Franz Ferdinand, fell in love with the Countess Sophie Chotek. She was a blue-blooded noblewoman of ancient Bohemian lineage, but a Hapsburg could not marry a commoner, even a Countess. The ominous birds at that time flew in screaming droves over Schonbrunn and the Hofburg Palaces, and they even followed the Imperial suite throughout the Empire.

Franz Ferdinand was sent on a trip around the world which lasted six years, but he could not put the beautiful Sophie Chotek out of his mind or life. The Emperor finally consented to a morganatic marriage, a union whereby the issue automatically would be deprived of all their hereditary rights, especially their right of succession.

Again the birds were seen and heard. Franz Ferdinand and his Sophie, however, did not heed the warnings, and were married July 1, 1900. For the first time it seemed the tradition of the ravens would fail, for the couple spent fourteen very happy years together.

On a lovely June day, Sophie, now Duchess of Hohenberg, was motoring in Vienna when she suddenly felt great excitement in the air. It was excitement tinged with terror, for great crowds were gathering on the sidewalks, looking fearfully toward the sky. Sophie ordered her chauffeur to draw the limousine up to the curb. She heard whispers from the crowd. "Turnfalken!"

She immediately changed her plans for the day and rushed to Konopischt in Bohemia, where her husband was in military conference with his aides. She entered the conference chamber unannounced. Knowing he planned to go to Sarajevo, Sophie pleaded with Franz Ferdinand to cancel his trip, but he and his men were adamant. She told him that the birds had been seen, that she herself had seen them, but Franz Ferdinand was a man who scoffed at superstitious fancies. Besides, he possessed one of those new bullet-proof vests. No harm could possibly come to him. Sophie's intuition knew better.

There was rebellion at Sarajevo. For centuries that part of the Hapsburg Empire had been seething with resentment against the rule of Austria-Hungary. When she realized that she could do nothing to dissuade her husband, she decided to accompany him and share his fate.

On June 28, 1914, the two motor cars of the Imperial party entered Sarajevo. A bomb was hurled at them by revolutionists, but no one was harmed. As the limousines approached the corner of Rudolph Street, a series of pistol shots rang out. Sophie fell across her husband's knees. He tried to speak to her, but blood was streaming from his mouth. Both Sophie and Franz Ferdinand were dying. The birds of the Hapsburgs had warned them as far back as 1894. This time the spectral warning had foretold the assassination and also the world catastrophe known as World War I.

The "White Lady" and the ravens of Europe's most powerful royal family had not manifested in vain.

A Little Bird Told Me

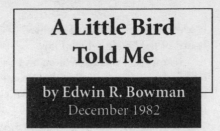

by Edwin R. Bowman
December 1982

On an April day in 1898 my mother, Eudora Bowman, raised a window to open the wooden shutter that had kept the bright sunlight out that morning. The moment she did so, an English sparrow flew into the room. Several days later, my four-year-old sister Eliva was badly burned when her dress ignited from the flames of a grate fire. She died two days later, on April 7.

In December 1911, when I was five years old, I became quite ill and was running a high temperature. The family doctor was visiting me twice a day. My mother moved me into my parents' bedroom where there was more room for the doctor and family members to move around. Although that was many years ago, I can still recall the huge red mahogany bed whose old-fashioned headboard almost touched the ceiling of the nine-foot-high room.

As I lay there burning with fever, my mother discovered that a sparrow somehow had gotten between the windowpane and the removable screen that served its purpose in the warm weather but that had not yet been stored for the winter months. Carefully, my mother raised the window a few inches so that she might open the screen and let the sparrow fly away, but instead of escaping, the bird flew into the room, circled it several times, and then alighted on top of the head-board of the bed in which I lay.

I suppose I was too young and too sick to see how terrified my mother suddenly became. She feared that the bird's appearance meant I wasn't going to recover from my illness.

We had no telephone, but my mother called to our next-door neighbor and asked her to send word to my father, Edwin Bowman, to come home from work as quickly as possible. Soon afterward, the family doctor made a hurried visit to see me. After examining me he declared that my condition had not changed.

That afternoon my mother received a telegram. It said her brother, Asa Bentley, who lived in Hollidays-burg, Pennsylvania, had died suddenly. Mother was saddened, of course, but at the same time she was greatly relieved that the omen had not presaged my death.

In September, 1920, my older brother, Henry, entered Richmond Medical College in Virginia. In early November, doctors found that he had a kidney ailment and he was sent to Stuart Circle Hospital in Richmond. After several weeks there he was returned to his home and to the care of the family doctor, but the specialist who had treated him in the hospital still visited Henry once or twice a week.

During this period, a male cardinal began to make frequent visits to Henry's window. It would perch on the sill practically every day and peck at its reflection in the glass. On December 20, Henry passed away and the cardinal never appeared at the window again.

In the summer of 1941, my other brother, Wallace, drove across the country to California, where he lived.

On his trip home he stopped in Estes National Park to visit the chief ranger, a friend of his. As he and the ranger were standing outside the latter's park house, a purple martin crashed against the picture window and dropped dead at their feet. The two men naturally assumed this was a normal wildlife accident.

But when he reached Cincinnati, Wallace found a message waiting for him. It urged him to change his route so he could visit our aunt, Marie Bentley, who was in the Allegheny Hospital in Cumberland, Maryland. He did visit her and a few days later, on August 5, she died. Had the martin in Estes National Park foretold her passing?

Through the years my family had many such experiences. Some of them, of course, remain more vividly in memory than others.

When my mother died on August 1, 1957, Wallace and I drove to Virginia for her funeral. On the evening of the day she was buried, our cousin, Lester Bowman, at whose home we were having dinner, said to us, "A strange thing happened to me a few days ago. I was driving to Richmond and a bird flew against my windshield and was killed."

I am sure that my cousin knew nothing of the family tradition of bird-omens, but when he told us what had happened, my brother and I exchanged knowing glances.

Another significant occurrence took place on September 5, 1959. My wife Cornelia and I, together with our daughter, Susan, and her friend, Marylou Mazurak, were returning to the Massachusetts mainland after a week's stay on Martha's Vineyard. The four of us sat on the upper deck of the ferry as it plied between Wood's

Hole and Oak Bluffs. We were chuckling at the antics of seabirds flying in a group some distance from us.

After a time, one of the birds left the irregular formation and flew directly toward our ferry. It followed closely for a time, changed its course briefly, then turned toward the vessel's stern. It repeated this course of action so persistently that we remarked how strange it was that the bird stayed with us rather than with its fellow gulls.

After disembarking from the ferry, we got into our car and drove the several hundred miles to our home in New York state. The next morning a telephone call from my brother informed me that Aunt Ida Bentley had died the previous day—the day that gull was trying to give us a message.

One month later Cornelia entered the hospital for treatment of a virus infection. She was an inpatient for four and a half weeks. The penicillin eventually licked the virus and my wife was scheduled to return home in a few days, but a cerebral hemorrhage caused her sudden death on October 28.

That evening I was talking with my son, Edwin Bowman III. He said, "Dad, there was no bird this time."

"Yes, there was," I replied. "This morning I was driving along Stratton Road and a bird flew upward against my car's radiator."

In August, 1969, I flew to California, rented a car and drove several hundred miles in that state. I visited Yosemite National Park on the fourteenth of the month and spent the day hiking along some of the shorter trails.

As I was climbing one steep trail, I became intrigued by the sight of a Steller's jay. I had never before seen a bird of this species and I was amused and fascinated by its behavior. It kept pace with me along the trail, flitting from bush to bush and from one sapling to another—always within a few feet of me. If I stopped, the bird stopped. When I resumed my progress, the jay also moved along. It even posed for me when I directed my camera toward it. That bird was good company.

Two days later I arrived at my relatives' home in Van Nuys, Calif. That day my son Ronald telephoned me from New York. He told me that my brother Wallace had just died. Did the Steller's jay know this was going to happen?

I could mention numerous other cases in which the appearances of birds were followed by deaths in my family. What such events mean I don't know. Perhaps some people would consider us superstitious, while others would say the supernatural directed those winged messengers.

Since I like to think we are not a superstitious family, I prefer to believe that the mystery can be explained as a series of coincidences. But who knows?

Amy Castile and the Hellhound

Bill Wharton
March 1958

Amy Castile stopped suddenly as she came around a bend in the narrow lane leading up to her home on the outskirts of Beccles in Suffolk, England.

Twilight shadows were just beginning to lengthen on this quiet spring evening in 1923, but the attractive sixteen-year-old schoolgirl had no eye for the leafy beauty around her.

Her normally calm blue eyes filled with terror as she stared at a part of the hedge bordering the lane about a dozen feet ahead of her.

She heard it again, a soft growl, and suddenly the head of an enormous hound emerged from the hedge.

For a second the girl and dog stared at one another, then the dog turned and padded quickly along the land toward the girl's house, as Amy emitted a piercing scream.

Terror-stricken, the girl burst into her mother's cottage. "I've seen it again!" she screamed. "The hellhound has been here again."

Mrs. Maude Castile tried to calm the girl. "There is no such thing as a hellhound, child," she admonished. "It is pure nonsense."

The girl looked up from the chair onto which she had thrown herself. "It is not nonsense, Mother," she replied. "This is the third time I have seen the same dog. Come and look; you must see its marks in the sand."

The woman and girl left the house to examine the lane and there, clearly imprinted in the fine dust, they saw the paw prints of a big dog.

The young girl was in such a state of nerves that she refused to leave her home at any time after sunset or to be out so late as to arrive home after sunset. To convince her daughter that she was imagining everything, Mrs. Castile called in the famous psychic investigator, Morley Adams.

Adams had heard about the "Hellhound of Beccles" but placed little faith in the story because he had never been able to find anyone who had actually seen this ghostly hound which was said to haunt this particular lane.

On receiving Mrs. Castile's letter, however, Adams decided to visit the lane and investigate. Shortly before his arrival Mrs. Castile and her daughter went to shops in the little neighboring town of Bungay and it was getting dark when they alighted from a bus near their home.

As they approached the lane, Amy Castile became agitated. Her mother took her hand as they entered the lane, but they had gone only a few steps when the terrified girl stopped.

"I hear it growl," she said. "It will appear now."

"You are silly, Amy," her mother snapped. "I can hear nothing."

"It is growling just like it did before Mrs. Jones died. I know someone is going to die. I can see the dog only when someone—"

She stopped suddenly and pointed a tremulous finger ahead of her. "There it is!" she screamed.

"I see nothing," her mother declared, gripping the frightened girl's hand.

"There by the holly hedge," Amy cried. Amy suddenly grasped her mother with her left hand—and instantly the older woman saw a massive black hound staring at them with slavering jaws and fangs bared.

Mrs. Castile, unfrightened, stared in disbelief because she could see the hedge right through the dog.

The dog turned, as Amy had previously described, and loped up the lane toward their house. Amy removed her left hand from her mother's arm and immediately the dog vanished from Mrs. Castile's sight, although the girl could still see it.

The next morning the mailman making his rounds told them that a neighbor, Mrs. Rupert Swift, had died in the night.

That same day Morley Adams arrived and began asking questions of people in the neighborhood. He talked with Amy Castile and her mother, and examined the lane where they had seen the dog. The paw prints were gone because a light rain had fallen in the night, but Adams discovered three men who also had seen the dog. In each instance some person living in the immediate area had died within twenty-four hours after the dog was seen.

These men had told no one about what they had seen because, they said, they did not want to seem foolish. Adams decided that he would try to see the hound for himself and spent six days waiting near the spot where the dog had appeared. He saw nothing.

He knew from experience that this might be a case where the hound appeared only on specific occasions, as when some person close by was about to die, or to a highly psychic person like Amy Castile. Talking the young girl into staying in the lane with him for an hour each evening at sunset was difficult, but she eventually agreed.

On the second evening the girl suddenly became tense next to Adams.

"I hear it," she whispered.

Adams heard nothing. When Amy Castile's terror-stricken eyes fixed on the holly hedge, Adams reached out with his left hand and closed it over the girl's left hand in a firm hold.

Instantly he saw a massive black hound, the largest he had ever seen, half emerged from the holly hedge. It was staring at them with bared fangs, and a low growl came to his ears.

He released the girl's hand and the dog immediately vanished, but as soon as he touched her hand he saw the dog again.

It came into the open and Adams, totally unafraid, realized he could see through it; the hound was completely transparent. It advanced a few paces toward the man and girl, then it turned and loped off up the lane.

Adams released his hold of the girl's hand and carefully examined the ground where he had seen the dog. There, clearly imprinted in the soft dust, was a set of prints made by the dog.

He took some photographs of the prints and that same night developed them, examining the still wet negatives under a light. In them he could see almost nothing, but when he took the negatives to a photographer the next day to be enlarged the faint impressions left by the dog's feet became visible.

Adams was satisfied that the dog was ghostly and that it came from one certain part of the holly hedge every time it was seen. With the help of a policeman he started investigating the glebe land behind the hedge the next day, prodding around until, toward afternoon, he found what he sought—a part of the ground which appeared to be richer in surface vegetation than the immediately surrounding land.

Digging down carefully, Adams had not got far when he came upon the remains of a Hessian sack, rotted away and containing the bones of a huge hound. He studied the bones, which he laid out above, but could find no trace of any bone injury which would account for the dog's death. The nature of the cord's knot around the opening of the sack told Adams a fuller story than the bones.

It was quite apparent to him that the dog had been put in the bag, the mouth of the bag securely tied, and the dog was buried alive.

It was not until months afterward that Adams discovered that some thirty years before a man named Askin had lived in the cottage where Amy Castile and her mother now resided. Askin had a six-year-old daughter. One evening while she was on the way home from a piano lesson she had been attacked by a neighbor's dog and so severely mauled that she died in the hospital.

Frantic with grief, Askin had insisted that the dog be destroyed, but, for some reason Adams could not fathom, the court had refused the order. Soon afterward the dog disappeared. It was thought that Askin had killed it, but the police were not particularly interested, and when no trace of it could be found, the matter was dropped.

For nearly thirty years the mystery of the vanished hound had remained unsolved. Its owner moved to another district and the whole matter was forgotten until Amy Castile and her mother came to live in the cottage.

Amy, Adams declared, proved to be a highly psychic girl, and her presence was enough to bring the asphyxiated hound from its grave. Once her overpowering psychic influence brought the dog from the dead, any person with some slight psychic influence could bring the dog back; thus other people also saw the dog. Even a person with no psychic influence whatever could see the ghostly hound if he touched Amy's hand.

Adams reinterred the dog's bones at another spot and for some months afterward kept in touch with the Castile family. Up to the time, five months later, when they moved from the area, Amy had not seen the dog again.

There has been no report since the girl's removal of anyone else having seen the dog known in Beccles and Bungay as the hellhound.

Animals and Humans

Anyone who has ever loved a pet knows the bond that can exist between a person and one of God's "lesser" creatures. Yet sometimes the barrier that separates man from beast breaks down and the relationship is fundamentally altered—and the bond of love manifests in surprising and inexplicable ways ...

Psychic Kinship of Man and Beast

Vincent H. Gaddis
November 1983

There is a strange psychic bond that human beings and animals share. This bond is most clearly demonstrated at death.

In December 1972, an Eastern Airlines jumbo jet plunged into the Florida Everglades, killing 100 passengers and crew. Among those fatally injured was Second Officer Don Repo, who lived for thirty hours after the crash.

Don Repo loved birds. Each morning he was home, he watched the birds at their feeder as he drank his coffee. A screened patio adjoined the kitchen.

Alice, Don's wife, usually kept the screen door slightly open to permit the dogs to come in or to go out. Occasionally, a bird or two would fly into the patio and she would use a broom to guide them back outside. Never had a bird found its way out without the aid of the broom.

On the day Don Repo died in a hospital, at least thirty birds appeared in the patio. They flew back and forth; then, without any guidance, they swept in a mass out the small opening to the outside.

"I said to myself, well, they all just came to say good-bye to Don," Alice told a reporter. "I just knew it because he loved birds so ... I'm convinced this was a kind of sign that Don was going to leave us."

Dr. E. H. McCleery, who almost single-handedly saved the lobo or buffalo wolves from extinction, kept a number of them on a Pennsylvania farm. His successor, Jack Lynch, was startled when, at noon one day, all the wolves howled "in a way he had never heard before and has not heard since." McCleery had just died.

Charles B. Hefelfinger loved life—all life. His pocket always bulged with candy for the children of the old Webster School in Bethlehem, Pennsylvania, where he was janitor. Here, too, a flock of pigeons descended for cracked corn. Some he called by name as they perched on him, pecking at his buttons or pulling out loose threads. Even on stormy Sundays he went to feed his birds.

When Charlie retired, they followed him to his home. They came at the same time and in that daily hour they belonged to him alone. When he was almost eighty, illness sent him to bed. Neighbors noticed then that his birds were sitting along the ridgepole of his house. They sat quietly, heads under their wings, waiting.

When Charlie's spirit was freed, the pigeons, responding to some strange signal, took flight. They knew that Charlie would never feed them again. They never came back.

There were also wild geese who "knew." The Gambill Wild Goose Reservation near Paris, Texas, was named for its founder, John Gambill. According to Joe F. Combs, feature writer for the *Beaumont* [Texas] *Enterprise,* Gambill once nursed a wounded honker back to health on his farm. Next autumn the gander returned, bringing twelve geese that became as tame as chickens.

The following year they came back a hundred strong. When Gambill gave his farm to the state, more than 2,000 geese wintered there in safety. During the winter of 1961–62, Gambill died in a Paris hospital—and as he was dying, to the bewilderment of doctors, nurses, and nearby residents, hundreds of geese flew over from the reservation and repeatedly circled the building, crying plaintively, honking their requiem.

Sometimes pets follow their masters in death. When Thomas A. Beasely of Peoria, Illinois, suffered a sudden heart attack, he collapsed on the floor of his bedroom and died shortly thereafter. Several hours later his pet collie, Lady, his inseparable companion for six years, scratched at the door of his room. Admitted by a member of the family, she crossed to the spot where her master had lain after his collapse and sniffed around uneasily. Suddenly she gave an odd cry and fell over on her side, dead.

At Jarrow-on-Tyne, Durham, England, there was a bird lover named William Milburn. From time to time he cared for wild birds, but during his twilight years only one was left—a song thrush that refused to fly away. She burst into melodious song whenever Milburn appeared and she would perch on his shoulders or atop his head as he walked about the house or in the yard.

When Milburn was stricken with influenza, the thrush sang very little. Milburn died early one morning. That day, and during the three days that the coffin was at the house, the bird did not sing at all.

When the day of the funeral arrived, the thrush was still silent, but as the pallbearers raised the casket to take it from the house, the bird began to sing more beautifully than ever before. Long and clear came the notes of her requiem as the procession moved away. When the hearse left for the church and cemetery, the thrush again lapsed into silence—this time forever. The following morning she, too, was dead.

In an interview with the late Hollywood columnist, Hedda Hopper, comedian Red Skelton told of two incidents that he would never forget. One had to do with his young son, Richard, who died of leukemia. Richard had several pets, but he was especially fond of a white billy goat. He used to say to the goat, "When I die I wish you'd go with me." The day after Richard died, the goat died.

Writer Gene Fowler was a frequent visitor at the Skelton home. During his visits he would play with and talk to a white cockatoo, of which he was fond. A few days before Fowler's death, Skelton heard him say to the bird, "I need your wings to take me where I hope to go." When Skelton came home from Fowler's funeral, the cockatoo was dead.

Occasionally, the affinity between an owner and a pet finds expression in a dream. Ignace Paderewski, renowned pianist and former premier of Poland, had a close friend: his parrot, Cocky Roberts. Whenever the master practiced, the parrot insisted on being present and, if shut out, would rap on the door with his beak, crying, "Cocky Roberts, let me in!" Although the bird's harsh voice was far from soothing to a sensitive ear, Paderewski never refused to admit his dictatorial pet.

Once inside, Cocky Roberts would perch on the pianist's pedal foot and ride with the music. Usually at the conclusion the parrot would exclaim, "Lord, how beautiful!" But occasionally he would squawk, "Lousy, lousy!" The great pianist said the bird's judgments were usually correct. In his memoirs Paderewski wrote, "That little bird had a soul."

Leaving Cocky Roberts in Switzerland, Paderewski came to America on tour. While in New York he saw his pet in a dream. "The entire night I dreamed of Cocky Roberts," he told friends the next day. "I dreamed about him and saw him, and I heard his funny, shrill, angry voice calling me—and it did not sound so unpleasant to me in the dream. And somehow I knew Cocky Roberts was dead and there was a very empty place in my heart."

Ten days later Paderewski received word that his parrot had died the same night he had dreamed of him. The night had been a bitterly cold one in Switzerland, and the bird had been accidentally left outdoors. The following morning his frozen body was discovered on the porch of the villa.

Sir Rider Haggard, the English author, had a similar experience. He dreamed that the family dog, a black retriever named Bob, was dying. The next day the dog turned up missing. After a search, the pet's body was found in a river below a railroad bridge. Inquiry revealed that the only train using that railroad branch had passed over the bridge at about the time of Sir Rider's dream and had apparently hit the dog.

The roots of our subtle affinities with animals extend deep into a remote past, back to a time when many animals, man among them, needed each other to survive the onslaughts of raging elements in a hostile world. Their affinity must have been very deep, and involved senses and abilities long lost.

Dr. Loren Eiseley, the prominent naturalist, says lingering legends indicate that the discovery of fire separated man from the animals. As men became organized into groups and tribes, the kinship continued with totems. The animals that symbolized the various totems were worshiped. In response to this outpouring of psychic energy, strange bonds were formed.

Totemism as an affective psychic power exists among some primitive peoples today. The anthropologist, Geoffrey Gorer, gives striking evidence of the psychic kinship between West African tribes in his book *Africa Dances*. Tribes around the Nyanza lakes have such animal kinships that should a boat be upset in crocodile-infested water, those who are of the crocodile totem swim slowly and unmolested to the shore; the others must beat off constant attacks at great peril.

Ronald Rose, a scholar who lived for a time among the Australian aborigines, writes in his book *Living Magic*, that among the more tribalistic natives the totem is a mediating vehicle for information. The appearance of the totem animal or bird announces that misfortune—in the form of an accident, illness, or death—has befallen another member of the totem clan.

As man developed his cultures, he lost contact with his animal brethren. He lost the mystical powers he once needed to survive as he created the artificial environments of civilization. Today man stands apart from the natural world, and the chasm between us and the rest of life is deep and wide.

A survival of ancient totemism may explain the mystery of the Gormanstown mourning foxes. The Gormanstown family is a very old one; the title is the second oldest of all the viscountcies of the British Isles, and goes back to the year 1478. Whenever a head of the house dies, beginning several hours before the death and ending only after the body is in the ground, all the foxes in the neighborhood come to the estate and surround the house. Why this happens, no one knows.

British-American writer Gerald Heard collected additional information from his own inquiries into the matter which the family had gone to some lengths not to publicize. A relative of his employed near Dublin became acquainted with the Earl of Fingall, the premier Catholic peer of Ireland and a man of scrupulous honesty. The Gormanstown manor is on the border of County Meath near Dublin, and the earl had once been master of the hounds with one of the most famous fox-hunting packs in all Europe, the Meath Hunt.

"A strange thing happened while I was Master of the Meath," Lord Fingall told Heard. "The Lord Gormanstown of that day died, and my huntsman told me that as long as the body was above ground there would be no use in drawing a covert. Naturally, no hunt was scheduled during this mourning period, but I considered the belief countryside superstition.

"As a Catholic dignitary, it was obligatory for me to attend the funeral, and it was proper for a funeral guest to enter the small domestic chapel alongside the house and pray by the coffin. When I walked to the chapel door it was dusk, and there on the steps sat two dogfoxes. To my astonishment, they showed no fear of me, but drew aside a few paces to allow me to enter. Naturally, I could ask no questions, but this experience ended my skepticism."

Several years later, Heard's employer in London, Sir Horace Plunkett, employed as one of his secretaries a male member of the Gormanstown family. Heard interviewed the man who, somewhat embarrassed, confirmed it was true that at each death of the head of the house, the foxes came into the manor grounds and prowled around the house until after the burial. No family member knew when or why it began; all anyone knew was that it was a happening of great age and no explanation.

As the mourning foxes came to the Gormanstown funerals, so do other animals attend their masters' final rites. Joseph Sproat, who had trained hundreds of pigeons since boyhood and held offices in the National Racing Pigeon Association, died in 1967. At his funeral in Calvary Cemetery in Pittsburgh, the mourners and an American Legion military salute team watched a flock of pigeons circle overhead and come to rest on a nearby hillside. When the services ended and the mourners were leaving, the birds flew from the hillside and came to rest on the unburied casket. They flapped their wings and cooed softly for a few minutes before flying away.

Telling bees of the death of their keeper, either by speaking aloud or by draping the hives in black crepe, is an Old World custom. It was introduced into New England in Colonial times. John Greenleaf Whittier wrote a poem about the practice. But how do we explain cases of bees attending funerals? (See "Telling the Bees," page 3.)

John Zepka of Adams, Massachusetts, was widely known in the Berkshires as an expert on beekeeping. Late in May 1956 he died. When the funeral cortege reached the grave, the mourners found the tent and floral sprays swarming with bees. Strangely, they remained immobile throughout the ceremony. Then they flew away.

A similar occurrence was reported by the Associated Press in April, 1961. When Sam Togers, postman at Myddle, Shropshire, England, died, his children walked around his fourteen hives and told his bees. During the graveside rites, the bees came by the thousands from Sam's hives, a mile away. Ignoring the flowering trees, they concentrated entirely on the funeral wreaths. The Reverend John Ayling said he had no explanation to offer. "Of course I try to rationalize such events," he said, "but if I didn't, I would say that those bees came to say good-bye to Sam."

Such occurrences, according to French parapsychologist Rene Sudre, suggest that communities of insects may have a collective psyche. "There is a soul of the hive," he writes. "A new entity emerges from the associations of individuals and rules their behavior."

There is another mystery. Do the minds of animals sometimes cross the gulf that separates them from the minds of human beings? What strange magnet of the heart can attract pets to the graves of those they loved?

When Harold King died in Nashville, he left behind a Scottie named Mac. A family friend took over ownership of the dog. Weeks later, in November 1951, Mac fell ill and was placed in the care of a veterinarian. One morning the dog disappeared. Two days later the caretaker of a cemetery found Mac's body on top of his late master's grave. What strange instinct told Mac he was about to die? And what strange beacon guided the dog to the grave miles from his new home?

At Kilda, near Melbourne, Australia, Mr. and Mrs. Robert King lived with their little girl and Mrs. King's elderly father, who had a cat named Felix. When the old gentleman died, Felix could not be comforted. He barely ate, and roamed the house and yard, searching and crying. The Kings found the cat's grief hard to bear in addition to their own, and to distract the pet they took him for an automobile ride. On the outskirts of Melbourne, they stopped at a traffic light.

Then something happened. Somehow Felix knew. He got to his feet, his coat bristling, and stood trembling for a few seconds, then sprang out the car's open window to the street. Dodging through traffic, he was soon out of sight. The family went home to wait for him, but he never came back.

Ten days later Mrs. King and her daughter went to the cemetery with some flowers. There, pacing back and forth on the grave, was Felix. As they approached, the cat became frantic with joy. He ran up to the little girl and began boxing with her just as he had done with the grandfather. Not only did this odd little game identify him, but he had the scar above one eye and the kink in a once-broken tail. Yet the cemetery was ten miles from their home and at least five miles from the place where the cat had jumped out of the car.

Twice before, they were ready to leave and got Felix as far as the cemetery gate, but each time he leaped out of the car. Mrs. King then arranged for the custodian to feed and care for the cat.

After reporter John Hetherington interviewed the family, he drove out to the cemetery. There was Felix, still pacing like a sentry, occasionally resting. Later Hetherington wrote, "This story haunts me. Perhaps it's because there are in it features that lie beyond the frontiers of human understanding."

In January 1972, three teenagers killed in a car-train collision at Midland, Texas were buried in Resthaven Cemetery. Several months after the burials, the cemetery custodian called Mrs. Max T. Brown and told her that an unidentified dog was sleeping beside the graves of her two daughters, who had died in the accident. As it turned out, Charlie Brown, the dog the two girls, Rebecca and Valerie, had owned, was missing. Mrs. Brown went to the cemetery and identified Charlie.

The custodian then noticed another dog sleeping on the grave of Jimmy McHargue, the third victim of the accident. Mrs. Brown recognized this second dog as Jimmy's Red. The cemetery was six miles away from their homes.

What is the secret of this mysterious rapport that sometimes manifests between man and his pets at trail's end? In his book *Between Two Worlds,* Nandor Fodor, the parapsychologist and psychoanalyst, suggests that those whom affection binds are, like the trees of a forest, always in contact below the level of consciousness.

"As the uprooting of a single tree is communicated to the other members of the sylvan community by the vibrations of the soil," he wrote, "so may the psychic earthquake of death reach one who loves and unite him, at the greatest crisis of life, with the object of his affection."

The Raccoons Who Came to Dinner

Ann Druffel
June 1985

In August 1956 my husband Charles and I moved our growing family from a mid-Los Angeles apartment to a hilly area in Eagle Rock, Calif. We both favored living in the hills rather than on flatlands of cement and blacktop.

Our new home on the rim of the San Gabriel Valley was in a wooded canyon which, though partially built up, still had a natural runoff stream during winter rains and much unimproved acreage with native flora and fauna. Wild trees, bushes, and other tangled vegetation were abundant. Although this small canyon was surrounded on three sides by heavily populated cities, wild animals shared our hills—coyotes, rabbits, squirrels, opossums, raccoons, and birds of all kinds, including jays, ravens, woodpeckers, and thrushes.

For the most part, the wild animals kept to themselves, and we caught glimpses of them only occasionally. A single jay, quickly named Mr. Blue Jay by our two older daughters, was bold enough to perch in nearby trees and entertain our little girls with raucous cries.

Southern California weather generally is mild and pleasant, even during summer. During the three hottest months of July, August, and September, the daytime temperature usually ranges from 80 to 90 degrees. At certain periods, however, the heat will unexpectedly "set record"; then there will be extended periods of a week or more when the thermometer soars above 100 at the Los Angeles Civic Center and reaches a blazing 105 to 115 degrees for several days at a time in the outlying valleys.

It was during such a streak of hot weather that a remarkable incident occurred. On September 28, 1963, at about 10:45 P.M., we were sitting in the living room of our hillside home, watching television and trying to ignore the heat. The high that day had been 107 degrees, and the thermometer still hovered around 100 degrees. The four days before had been nearly as hot, and our house, unlike the houses of some of our more affluent neighbors, had no air conditioning or swimming pool. We were tired of the heat and our nerves were wearing thin. Our daughters, who now had multiplied to four, were sound asleep.

Suddenly, over the din of canned laughter from a TV sitcom, we heard a scratching at our front door, which faced onto an acre of tangled wildwood west of our home. Thinking it was a neighbor's dog, we ignored the noise. The scratching persisted, and after a minute or two I opened the door to see what was causing the sound.

To my astonishment I saw a large raccoon standing less than two feet from me, gazing intently into my eyes. She showed no fear, only an air of caution as she beseeched me silently with her large brown eyes. I looked beyond her in the faint glow which our dim indoor lighting cast on our darkened porch.

Several feet away I saw, positioned on the edge of the shallow steps which led to our driveway—and beyond that, to the wild acreage—three small raccoons which could not have been more than a few months old. They were clustered on the broad stairs, poised as if ready to flee on a signal from the large raccoon. There was an air of expectancy and urgency about them—an attitude they seemed to have picked up from the large raccoon, which apparently was their mother.

I called softly to Charlie to come and see what was on the porch. When he came to the door and peered out, his surprise matched mine. Together we gazed at the mother raccoon. At least one foot high and two feet long, she was as big as a fair-sized dog. Never had we seen a raccoon so close and so unafraid. We had seen raccoons in our area, but they had always scampered off as if unwilling to have anything to do with human beings.

The mother raccoon looked steadily and intensely at us. Even in her urgent plea, she never lost her air of caution. She kept looking toward the three small babies and then back at us.

Charlie and I both suddenly realized that the mother raccoon was telling us that the intense heat of the past four days was affecting her babies adversely. We thought of food and water, especially water; our streambed had been dry for months. Charlie filled a large pan of water and carefully placed it on the porch midway between the mother and her babies. The large raccoon just as carefully moved aside so that Charlie could go out the door.

The raccoons stared silently at the water. Then the mother went over and sniffed at it. She returned immediately to her place near us; her babies did not go near the water. We decided it wasn't what the mother was requesting so urgently. Years later I realized that they probably could not tolerate the heavy chlorination for which Los Angeles County water is famous.

Charlie went to the refrigerator and, perhaps instinctively, brought out a large bowl of juicy green grapes which we had purchased that evening for our children to enjoy the next day. He placed a small clump of the grapes on the porch near the water. The mother drew near the grapes, nosed them carefully, then called to her babies with the sharp cry peculiar to raccoons.

The babies hurried over and—as if by their mother's permission—hungrily gobbled down the grapes. The mother once more beseeched us; she was asking for more grapes. We provided large clumps of them and the babies swiftly consumed them. The mother did not eat even one grape. Apparently she was saving everything for her babies.

By this time Charlie and I had silently decided to let our own children witness this strange but charming spectacle. I went upstairs and gathered our own brood, four small girls aged eight to one-and-one-half years. I exacted from each a stern promise to be very quiet. Although normally noisy and playful, they stood as quiet as little mice at the door, watching the baby raccoons gulp down clump after clump of juicy grapes, provided by their daddy, at the silent direction of a large mother raccoon. The wonder in our small children's eyes was a marvel to behold—akin to the marvel of the gratitude in the mother raccoon's eyes.

While the babies were eating the grapes, the mother stood a short distance away from us. When our children joined the group, she took up a position nearer her babies. Her attitude was that of a wary guard, alert although still trustful.

It appeared that the juicy fruit was alleviating both the raccoon's hunger and thirst. When the grapes were completely consumed, we tried laying out bits of cut-up bananas, but the mother, after sniffing this offering, rejected it. She gathered her babies and, with a final look of what seemed close to gratitude, the little group turned and shuffled off into the darkness of the wildwood.

The entire episode lasted about fifteen minutes, and was an unprecedented experience for all of us—one that has never occurred since. The heat wave broke a couple of days later. On the 30th the high was a "mere" 99 degrees. Our family felt better, not only for ourselves but also for the raccoons.

Our children looked for them for days afterward, hoping they would return for another meal, but we never saw that particular family again. In years that followed, we often saw raccoons wandering at night among the bushes and trees near our home, and sometimes strolling boldly down our driveway. We learned they are nomadic and not inclined to stay long in one place. Strangely, subsequent visiting raccoons show no fear, at least of Charlie and me. They treat our place as their own property, but do not interact with us in any unusual way.

We have always felt that the desperate circumstances of hunger and thirst the raccoons must have endured that hot summer sparked the trust that allowed the mother to approach us and ask for help. But did the fact that we also had small "babies" have anything to do with her decision to scratch on our door that night? She might have chosen any of a dozen homes along that winding street, but we were the only family in our glen to have children so young.

This is something, of course, that we will never know, but we feel privileged to know from our experience that sometimes, under unusual circumstances, wild animals do communicate with human beings.

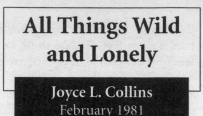

All Things Wild and Lonely

Joyce L. Collins
February 1981

I wasn't anybody special. No more and no less intelligent than any child my age. I was basically a normal seven-year-old girl although perhaps more shy and lonely than most.

In 1935, I went to my grandmother Ethel Tucker's farm near Brighton, Iowa, to spend the summer vacation from school. There I would sit on the porch and watch a wild stallion named Ruby in the pasture at the neighboring farm, owned by a Mr. Reese. Mr. Reese warned everyone in the area to stay away from that horse, because the animal had already killed one man who tried to rope him and put another man in the hospital with a broken back.

Knowing how much I loved animals, everyone warned me repeatedly to stay away from Ruby. Although I had never been near him, Grandmother often expressed concern to others that I might try to pet the "wild one" and something terrible would happen.

Ruby was a beautiful, blue-black, sleek-coated animal, and I thought he acted afraid and lonely. People said he was wild because he came straight off the range from a wild herd.

I watched him rear up on his hind legs, whinny and paw at the ground. A daydreamer, I began pretending to be inside the horse's body to absorb his feelings.

I wanted to be his trusted friend, and imagined myself petting him and loving him as my very own pal. As I let my mind wander inside his body, I sensed confusion. Ropes snared him and took him away from the range and his family. Human beings fenced him in, whipped him, and denied him his freedom. Loneliness engulfed him there in his empty pasture with the high fence.

Two weeks later, I noticed that whenever I went to the porch to watch him my thoughts inevitably followed the path toward the pasture where he was. I imagined myself reaching up and touching his cheek and petting him.

Then he suddenly stopped pawing the ground and looked directly toward me. I imagined myself talking with him as if I were standing beside him.

Every day at three o'clock in the afternoon was rest time at Grandmother's house. I always chose to sit on the porch so that I could watch Ruby and "talk" with him inside my head.

He started coming to the fence nearest the house when he saw me come out on the porch. He nickered softly, as if acceding to my silent wish that he be my very own. Together we would never be lonely again. He seemed somehow to understand.

Before the summer was over, Ruby and I became close friends. One day my grandmother had to go somewhere and she told me to go over and play with Wilma, who lived on a neighboring farm. Grandma looked out the door to see where the wild horse was before she would allow me to walk past the pasture alone.

I told her good-bye, and I started down the lane that ran past the pasture. I kept thinking, "Touch, love, touch," as I walked, and the sensation of touching Ruby's face was strong in my mind.

I saw the horse look in my direction and he started slowly toward me. Then he broke into a gallop and stopped at the fence that separated us.

I held out my hand and Ruby stretched his neck as far as he could, reaching toward my hand. He nickered low. I could barely reach the tip of his nose. The barbed wire of the fence bit into his flesh as he reached toward me even farther.

"Ruby, I love you," I whispered. "I wish you was mine. I wouldn't let you be lonely." My childish promise was heartfelt, and Ruby lowered his head so that I could put my hand through the bottom portion of the fence and touch his cheek.

This was the first time I was near him and the first time I had spoken to him aloud. I was thrilled beyond words because he seemed to know me.

Thoughts flashed in my mind of what would happen if my grandmother caught me so near the "wild one." Apologizing to Ruby, I hurried toward Wilma's house.

As the summer ended and I was preparing to return home to start school in the fall, my grandmother wanted me to go to the store. She took the milk pail and started toward the barn to milk the cow as she told me to hurry past the pasture. I knew she couldn't see me from the barn, so I raced down the lane.

Ruby galloped toward me and stopped at the fence.

"I have to go home tomorrow, Ruby," I said, tears streaming down my face as I touched him. "I don't want to because I can't see you anymore. I have to go to the store. You wait here and I will talk to you on my way back."

I rushed to the store, made the purchases and ran most of the way back so that I could have a little time with Ruby before my grandmother expected me home.

Ruby was still standing by the fence as I approached him.

"Oh, Ruby, I don't want to go," I said. "Maybe I will never see you again." I cried. He was reaching for me and I put my face up close to the fence. He nuzzled my neck as if trying to whisper in my ear. "Good-bye, Ruby. You be good and remember I'll always love you no matter where I am."

I walked slowly up the lane toward the house.

I returned home to Buffalo, Iowa, and tried to settle down to my schoolwork, but my heart was with Ruby. Thanksgiving came and Grandmother arrived for a visit. She and Mother were conversing when I heard Grandmother mention the "wild horse." I stopped to listen.

"You know Mr. Reese, the farmer who owns that wild horse I was telling you about?" she asked.

Mother nodded.

"He told me a few days ago that he didn't know what happened to that horse, but it was gentle now. He didn't know if keeping him in that pasture alone all summer did the job or not, but something sure tamed him down. He is so darn proud of that horse now he never stops talking about him."

Although I kept still, my heart was bursting with happiness because now I knew Ruby would never have to be afraid or lonely again. I never told anyone I had anything to do with him. Who would have believed me?

The following year, Grandmother moved to a farm on the other side of Brighton. She had written Mother that she felt as if she had moved into the past. Wild range cattle foraged in the underbrush and trees toward the rear of her farm, but she added they would not come close to the house or outbuildings.

That summer I went to my grandmother's again for a visit.

At first opportunity I headed "for a walk" toward a grove of trees where I sat on a tree stump and watched for the wild cattle she had told us about.

When I saw them in the distance, I noticed it was a small herd. The animals seemed peaceful as they grazed. Something startled them and they ran in my direction. They stopped about half a mile from me, unaware of my presence, and began to grazed again.

The love in my heart for these poor half-starved creatures no one wanted made me wish I could communicate my feelings to them. I wondered what frightened them, what they were thinking, and what they were feeling. I thought about the lead cow. Once it raised its head and looked in my direction. I continued to think about how I would like to know its feelings and thoughts. Each day they seemed to be more curious about me. The lead cow ventured nearer and in a few days it came so close to me that I could almost reach out my hand and touch it.

I daydreamed again, just as I had with the stallion, and imagined myself inside its body. When I did, I felt tired and wanted to lie down. I kept thinking this over and over again, and soon the lead cow lowered its head and its frail-looking body slumped to the ground.

I wasn't paying a lot of attention to the others at the moment. The one now lying on the ground in front of me watched me and chewed its cud while the frightened look in its eyes seemed to disappear.

Suddenly I heard heavy breathing behind me. I turned slowly and saw three more standing with their heads down, sniffing my hair.

I thought how tired they looked and they too lay down. It wasn't long until the rest of them lay on the ground around me.

I had not spoken to them aloud, but after they began coming to me the moment they saw me each day, I waited until they lay on the ground; then I spoke to them for the first time.

I told them I wanted to be their friend. I wanted them always to trust me because I would never harm them.

When the summer ended and I was planning to return home, I went out to talk to my little herd just one more time.

As they grouped around me, I told them I had to go away. I held out my hand to the lead cow and its big rough tongue licked my hand. I started to walk way with tears in my eyes, because I didn't know if I would ever see them again.

I heard a rustling sound behind me and when I turned to look, I saw ten head of wild cattle walking slowly behind me.

I had to walk a quarter mile through the trees to a clearing before I came to the edge of my grandmother's property. Periodically, I turned and watched those poor animals following me. They were a pitiful sight.

When I came within shouting distance of the farm, I saw my uncle, Kenneth Hollenbeck, who was seventeen or eighteen at the time, by the barn and I heard him call to Grandmother, "Look yonder."

Startled, the cattle stopped dead in their tracks and looked around nervously as though trying to decide whether to stay or stampede. I talked to them calmly and told them no one would harm them. I patted the lead cow on the face.

I waved to my uncle. He frantically motioned for me to get away from the wild herd.

I turned again to my friends. They stood very still as I walked among them. The lead cow seemed always to be beside me as I touched each of them on the face in farewell.

As they gathered around me, they towered above my small body so that I couldn't see over them. I wanted to know what my uncle was doing. I was afraid that if he came after me I would get the whipping of my life.

I didn't see him, so I continued to tell my friends I was going away and I couldn't see them again for a long time. I touched each of them with the pure, true love of a child.

I walked toward the barn and I turned once to get one more look at the precious little herd of cattle. They were standing where I had left them, watching me. The lead cow mooed softly.

My uncle ran to me, scolding me severely, telling me that I could have been killed because those were wild range cattle that no human hand had ever touched. If they stampeded, I would not have had a chance.

I didn't say anything. He would never believe these wild critters were my dear friends.

Perhaps it was this incident that caused Mother to decide not to allow me to return to Grandmother's house. I stayed home the next two summers. I never saw my special herd again.

When I was ten years old, we moved to another house in Buffalo. This one was located on the banks of the Mississippi River. I knew that snakes live along riverbanks and I was terrified of the reptiles. Mother warned me to beware of them.

That summer I saw my first movie. One of a series about Sabu, the Elephant Boy, it had a scene in which Sabu spoke to a huge snake. It made a great impression on me.

The next day was Sunday. After my chores were done, I went out into the yard and sat in the big willow lawn chair and propped my feet up in another chair.

I couldn't get the movie out of my mind. I thought about how it would be to communicate with animals of all kinds, just as Sabu had. I was envious. I thought about what it would be like to not be terrified of snakes.

I sat in the chair with my head leaned against the back for an hour or more. I closed my eyes and day-dreamed about snakes. I wondered if they had a mind like other animals. I wondered what it was like to be a snake, what snakes thought of human beings, if they can understand the emotions of people who fear them.

Suddenly, I thought I saw a movement out of the corner of my eye, but I paid no attention to it. I was caught up in my daydream. Then I noticed the movement again. Still I paid no heed. The third time I felt a slight bump against the leg of my chair and when I looked I screamed.

Pressed against the leg of my chair was the largest water moccasin I had ever seen!

Mother appeared at the door and I shouted, "Snake!"

Running to the woodshed, she got the garden hoe. As she inched her way toward me, she quietly instructed me to stand up in the chair just as she made her first strike at the snake; then I should jump off the other side away from the snake and flee to the house.

But I couldn't move. I froze.

I stared down at the monstrous snake so close to me. Then a strange feeling swept over me, a sensation that told me this snake meant no harm, that it did not intend to frighten or hurt me.

Mother killed the snake after a terrible battle. She stretched its body across our eight foot driveway. Its head touched one side of the driveway and its tail overlapped the other side by about 10 inches, which meant the snake was almost nine feet long!

Old-timers who had lived near the Mississippi all their lives said they had never seen a water moccasin this big.

Many years later, as an adult familiar with the concept of ESP, I wondered if I had mentally called the snake. I have felt bad about this, because if that is the case the snake lost its life for answering me.

But when I was young, I had no idea what I was doing—why a killer horse trusted me, why wild range cattle put their faith in me, or why such a huge snake should take that particular moment to make its presence known. Was it simply a coincidence that the movie snake, the one I was daydreaming about, was an unusually large one, and the one that came to me in reality was similarly an oversized one?

I am over fifty years old now, and I have come in contact with many wild animals in the years since then, yet none have ever seemed afraid of me and I have never been attacked or bitten by any of them.

The Kid Must Have Been Dreaming

Violet M. O'Brien
September 1979

My dog was dying! As we were playing, she had leaped over a barbed wire fence and slashed her belly open. I was only six years old, and the sight of blood spreading a stain over Smokey's soft white underside frightened me. I felt sick.

I rushed home through the dry field. Mom was just leaving for town. She patted my shoulder and promised to have Jim, our neighbor, come over. I was crushed. My dog was dying and nobody cared. I ran back to Smokey, and a few minutes later I felt a hand on my shoulder and looked up at the tall rangy figure of Jim Pedersen. He leaned over, gently picked up Smokey, and headed for his house. I ran home sobbing and hid behind the house.

Then through my tears, I peered around the corner and saw Jim putting my dog into the seat of his truck. I sat on the steps and watched the dust swirling behind the truck as it took off down the road.

Then it seemed I was in the truck cradling Smokey's head in my lap, rubbing her ears and trying to keep my eyes off the terrible gaping wound. Jim didn't say a word.

We pulled into the parking area. Jim took Smokey and walked toward the oblong light-yellow building. Following him through the door, I sidled into one of the chairs lined up against the wall. A little dog kept yapping;

162

a guinea pig held by a little girl squealed repeatedly. I could hear the yelping of dogs down the dark corridor to my right. Jim talked with the vet and carried Smokey through another door. I glimpsed white walls inside as the door swung closed. I cried silently.

Soon Jim came out with the vet. They were talking. I saw Jim take out his wallet—and the next thing I knew, I was sitting on the steps of our house and Mom was driving in.

A few days later I went with Mom to pick up Smokey. I showed her the way, and even though I had been told I did not go with Jim that day, I knew the parking lot, I knew the building, I knew the office, I knew I had been there before.

Even now, over thirty years later, with a university degree in science and numerous courses in logic and scientific methods behind me, I remember vividly that trip to the vet's office with Jim and Smokey—the trip I never made.

On a warm summer's day in 1945 our six-year-old son Denis came running into the house.

"Smokey cut her stomach open and all her insides are falling out!" he shouted. "She jumped over the barbed wire fence!" His face was white and he was sobbing uncontrollably. Smokey was his dog and his whole life.

I had bought a home with an acre of ground, two miles from Medford, Oregon, thinking it would be a better place for our three boys while their dad served overseas during World War II. It had helped the older boy, Richard and Patrick, but not Denis, a quiet little boy who harbored intense feelings about anyone he loved. He felt his father's absence keenly and his canine friend became the focus of his affection.

"How could she do that?" I asked Denis. Even though he kept on sobbing, I was sure it wasn't that serious. I remembered how upset he had become when as a puppy Smokey loved to hang onto his pants leg and invariably broke a tooth. Once Denis rushed inside with the tooth-filled jaw of a rodent, positive it belonged to Smokey. It had taken me an hour to prove to him that his dog's teeth were intact.

Not terribly concerned, I told Denis I was in a hurry but would ask our neighbor Jim Pedersen to take care of it.

Jim, who had three children of his own, was very good with boys and animals. He was out fixing a fence when I drove up and explained Denis' problem. He dropped his work immediately and left for the house. Relieved, I tried to push the slight feeling of guilt out of my mind for not taking the time to check on Smokey's condition.

I thought of the time I had brought the dog home. An Australian shepherd type, hardly more than a big ball of fluff, she won Denis' heart and the two became inseparable. As the dog grew out of puppyhood, she seemed to take on Denis' personality. They seemed to be of one mind, and both reacted the same way to any given circumstance. If I scolded the boy he quietly went behind the house and hid for an hour or two; if I scolded Smokey she did the same thing.

Denis was the only one who could feed her. He would lie on the grass for hours watching her, a soft smile on his face while the dog stood like a statue, her little flag-like tail waving rapidly back and forth, her eyes glued to the ground, hypnotized by the flickering shadows made by the leaves of a tree or a butterfly.

On that day when the dog jumped over the fence I was already late for a dental appointment. During the war years it was almost impossible to get an appointment and I couldn't afford to miss this one.

When I returned Denis was sitting on the steps. His face was streaked with tears; he was the picture of dejection.

I sat beside him and held him close. "How's Smokey?" I said.

"She had to have thirteen stitches," he answered, his voice breaking into sobs.

"Where is she?" I asked softly. I felt that I had let the boy down when he needed me.

"In the dog hospital." He covered his face. "Doctor said she would have to stay there for a while."

"That's going to cost money. Do you know how much?"

Denis looked at me. "I think Jim paid," he said. "I saw him take out his wallet but a little dog kept barking and I couldn't hear what he said." He began to sob again.

"Were there any other animals there?" I said, hoping to take his mind off Smokey.

He broke into a small smile and his eyes glistened through his tears. "A little girl had a guinea pig." He laughed softly. "Every time the dog barked it squealed real loud." For a moment he was happy, remembering.

"Is Smokey at the same place we took her for shots?"

"No, it's on the other side of town. Jim thought it was better than the other one." He began to cry again. "There's blood all over the truck seat."

I examined Denis' clothes but there was no blood on them. I hugged him and said, "Don't worry. I'll go talk to Jim, and maybe tomorrow we can go and see Smokey." He gave me a flicker of a smile and nodded.

I went over to see our neighbor, whom I found unloading some bags from his truck. "How much do I owe you, Jim?" I asked.

He shook his head. "Nothing," he replied. "The doc said to pay it all when you pick the dog up. She'll have to stay for a few days."

"But Denis said he saw you take out your wallet."

Jim looked perplexed. "I did—but how did he know? He didn't go with me. He ran around to the back of your house. He was very upset. I didn't want to take the time to go after him because I knew Smokey needed attention right away."

"Denis said Smokey had to have thirteen stitches. You must have told him."

"I just got back—haven't seen Denis," he said. "Made a couple of stops on the way home." He shook his head again. "Smokey did have thirteen stitches. Kid must have been dreaming."

By then I was completely confused. "You took her to the animal clinic on the other side of town?"

Jim frowned and glanced at me as if I had lost my mind. "Yes," he confirmed. "I know the vet there and he's really good. Smokey will be fine in a couple of days."

"Were there any other animals in the waiting room?" I realized I was sounding more foolish all the time.

Jim laughed. "Yes, a little black poodle barking its head off," he said. Then he added, "Oh, there was a little girl with a guinea pig. It squealed so loud I couldn't hear myself think."

"I know," I mumbled. "Denis told me."

"Don't know how he could. He sure didn't go with me."

I thanked him and left. I was trembling. Walking past Jim's truck I didn't want to look, but I knew I had to. The seat was covered with blood!

"Haven't had time to wash it off," Jim called over to me. "Don't worry about it."

I hurried home to Denis who was still sitting on the steps looking forlorn. My heart went out to him but I knew there was nothing I could do to ease his pain. I took him in my arms and held him. "What color was the little dog that barked so much?" I asked him. I had already divined his answer but had to hear him say it.

"Black and curly all over," he whispered.

"Did you go with Jim?" I held my breath.

He stared at me for a moment, a confused frown on his face. "No, but I saw it," he said uncertainly. Then he added, "I don't know if I did."

I decided not to press him. He'd had enough emotional upset for one day. A few months later, however, I asked him the same question and got the same answer.

From that time on I have tried to find a rational answer to the strange event. Did a child's intense love for his dog enable him to accompany his pet mentally while physically he stayed at home?

Smokey survived her ordeal and lived to a ripe old age. Denis is a grown man now with a family of his own but he still remembers the day he went to the veterinarian with his dog. We never cease to wonder about that strange and wonderful event.

I Came Back for My Dog

Barbara C. Powell
June 1986

As a professional psychic, I am interested in the many kinds of paranormal experiences people report. One of the most unusual incidents I have ever heard about occurred in Wendover, Utah, in January 1963.

Joe Benson was a spiritual leader to the Goshute Indians. One day, while visiting one of the local markets in Wendover, he found a stray puppy, weak and pitiful but full of the life spirit. Recognizing this as a bond between them, the old man took the dog home.

He nursed it on venison broth and mixtures of native herbs which healed and strengthened the animal. Then, as the dog got better, he named him Sky, because in his culture the sky held the greatest strength. Soon the old man and his dog could be seen making regular rounds from the high sheep meadows to the corrals where the younger men of the family broke horses for neighboring ranchers.

By the time the winter came to the pine and sage country, the dog had grown to become a magnificent German shepherd of apparently pure lineage.

Sky had only one master, He was reserved and sometimes—rarely—friendly with others, but he loved only the old man who had saved him. As Mr. Benson grew older and his vision failed him, the dog guarded his steps. His family worried about him because they sensed that more than his eyes had weakened. Still, they felt sure that Sky would watch him and keep him from harm.

Finally Joe Benson went to his wife Mable and announced that his time was near. She sent word to the relatives. The children, grandchildren, nephews, and nieces all came to the old man's bedside. Because they were more involved in white society than he was, they ignored his protests and insisted he be moved to the Indian Hospital in Owyhee, Nevada. Sky growled when they lifted him, and cried when they took him away.

The old man did not last long in the hospital. He asked that the nurses place him in a chair each day so that he could look down the valley in the direction of his home. At last, knowing that Joe Benson was beyond their care, they sent him home to Wendover to die. In deep winter, in January, 1963, he died.

The funeral celebration lasted several days. Singers came and sang to his soul for three nights. Other wise and holy men came to contribute their chants. Finally at the dawning of the fourth day, the people were quite sure that his soul had passed beyond. Quietly they ate the huge breakfast that was prepared for them, and just as quietly they left. Soon only Mable was left in the house, alone with her memories and Joe's dog Sky.

Before they left the little town in Utah, several people, children, grandchildren, and the old man's friends, had asked for the dog. The old woman thought about it—the dog, which seemed to be grieving even more than she was, filled the house with his sorrow—but she sensed that that would be the wrong thing to do. So she kept the dog.

About ten days later she happened to look out the window to see a man coming up her road. She built up the fire in her old cookstove and put on the coffee for her guest. The coffee was just heating up when she saw her visitor in the doorway. Her hand trembled, but she did not drop the coffeepot. She placed it on the stove and turned back to face him. It was Joe.

True to the traditions of her people, she gently explained to him that he was dead, that he had no business in the land of the living and that he had to pass on. This world was closed to him.

Joe nodded. "I am going," he said. "I just came back for my dog." He whistled and called and Sky came running into the kitchen. He wagged his tail, then sat down expectantly. "I want his leash," Joe said to Mable.

Mable went to a hook on the wall and took it down. She handed it to him, making sure that she did not touch him.

Grandfather snapped the leash on Sky's collar and led the dog away, across the porch, down the steps and along the familiar path around the hill. Not once did he turn back even to wave to his wife; not once did he say good-bye.

Mable hesitated for a moment, then ran after him. When she reached the turn of the hill and looked, there was nothing. Joe and Sky were gone.

Joe and Mable's daughter, Arvilla Benson Urban, who lived next door to them, saw this happen and has sworn to it in an affidavit. In late January 1963, she says, "I saw my father enter the house, and not more than a few minutes later I saw him leave with the dog on a leash. I saw my mother go after him and I, after I could think, went after her.

"When I reached the top of the hill, my father and his dog were gone."

The young men of the family spent several days searching for the dog. No trace of him or of his leash was ever found.

All of those who had asked for the dog were later thankful that they hadn't taken him. They would not have wanted Joe to come to their house asking for Sky.

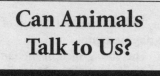

Can Animals Talk to Us?

D. Scott Rogo
January 1981

I was standing in a Los Angeles pet store, trying to nudge a recalcitrant myna bird into talking to me while a few of my friends looked on disparagingly. Despite all my efforts, the bird would not speak. The cat had gotten its tongue, it seemed, and I was beginning to wish that the feline had taken the rest of the bird as well. Finally I had to call it quits.

"Is there a back entrance to this place?" I asked the store manager.

The bird perked up.

"Out through the back," the manager replied.

"And shut the door when you leave," squawked the myna bird.

The command was so apropos that all of us, including the store manager, burst out laughing. It was hard to believe that the bird had no real awareness of what it had said, but in fact was only mimicking word sounds. We were the ones who had found meaning in them.

Those of us who love animals like to anthropomorphize our feathered and furry friends. We tend to endow them with human emotions; we like to think they are motivated by intelligence and feelings when they act toward us with either love or anger. But are our animal friends really thinking when they respond to us? This question is now being asked by animal behaviorists engaged in the study of animal communications and "semiotics."

Semiotics is the study of "signing"—communication by direct or indirect signalling and cuing. It is a field that is evolving rapidly because of new studies which purport to prove that nonhuman primates (such as chimpanzees and gorillas) can be taught "language" and communication skills. Some researchers hold that animals can be taught to use sign language or to press buttons representing words on a computer terminal. Ape "signing" studies are now being conducted at several American universities and have recently engendered one of the hottest debates in contemporary psychology.

Perhaps the most famous of these studies began thirteen years ago when Beatrice and Allen Gardner, two researchers at the University of Nevada, succeeded in teaching a female chimpanzee named Washoe more than 100 words in American sign language. Washoe has become something of a celebrity and has been featured on Public Broadcasting System's "Nova" program, as well as in several documentaries. More recently, David Premack (who until lately worked at the University of California-Santa Barbara) taught another chimpanzee to communicate using plastic chips, each of which symbolized a different word.

The most exciting work in the field is that of Dr. Duane Rumbaugh and Sue Savage-Rumbaugh, who have taught a female chimp named Lana to communicate over a computer terminal at the Yerkes Regional Primate Research Center at Emory University in Atlanta, Georgia. The Rumbaughs' work is also probably the most controversial of all the recent research on man-animal communication. They are now claiming that, having taught their chimps simple words and word associations, the animals have begun spontaneously to compose sentences in a meaningful way, just as children do!

The work of these two researchers has not gone unchallenged. Their research and that of other animal behaviorists working with man-animal communication has been strongly criticized by Dr. Thomas Sebeok, an anthropologist at Indiana University in Bloomington. He has argued that the Rumbaughs are deluding themselves, "reading into" the chimps' utterances meanings that aren't there—just as I was tempted to do when the myna bird told me to shut the door in that Los Angeles pet store. Worse still, Sebeok claims that many animal behaviorists are inadvertently "cuing" their animals, unintentionally signaling them into giving allegedly meaningful responses.

So who's right? Can apes communicate with us or can't they?

To answer this question, the New York Academy of Sciences held a symposium on May 6 and 7, 1980, at the Roosevelt Hotel in New York City. Dr. Sebeok was a prime mover in getting the symposium under way and the very title of the conference reflected his bias toward the subject of communicating animals: it was titled "Conference of the Clever Hans Phenomenon."

"Clever Hans" is the name of a wonder horse who was trained about the turn of the century by William von Osten, a German animal trainer, to answer mathematical questions by tapping his foot. No one could figure out how the horse could come up with so many correct answers to sometimes complicated problems until Oskar Pfungst, a Prussian psychologist, journeyed to Berlin to study the horse at first hand. He discovered that von Osten was actually cuing the horse, subtly and quite accidentally, by tilting his head when he wanted the horse either to start or to stop tapping his foot. Clever Hans didn't really know what he was doing; he had just learned to watch his trainer for the right signals in order to get a piece of carrot of other reward. The mystery of "Clever Hans" was solved and Pfungst even demonstrated that he himself could make the horse start and stop counting.

Since the explanation of the "Clever Hans phenomenon," animal behaviorists have had to guard against falling into a similar trap when studying animal intelligence. According to Sebeok, Rumbaugh and his colleagues are enthusiastic victims of the Clever Hans trap. But can such a simple phenomenon account for the fact that the Rumbaughs' chimps and other communicating apes seem to be learning how to use their limited language skill by stringing together original word combinations and composing direct requests for specific foods and other sought-after objects?

I was just as confused as anyone else interested in animal psychology when I flew to New York to attend the meeting which was held to discuss this issue. I naively thought that the conference would help to resolve the debate, but I soon learned that the question can be argued equally well either way.

One of the key issues raised at the conference was whether communicating apes have in fact learned to string words together in an orderly fashion spontaneously, without special training by their human mentors. Several conference participants believe they have. Perhaps the best-known and oft-cited example of this concerns Washoe. One day while boating with her trainer, she was shown a swan. When asked what the bird was, Washoe gave the sign for "water" followed by the sign for "bird." Thus, according to her trainer, Washoe had invented the word "waterbird." The trainer had expected her to give only the sign for "bird" and was stunned by her originality. On another occasion Washoe was angry when her trainer (Roger) wouldn't take her for a walk and signed "dirty Roger." As "dirty" was the sign Washoe had learned for excretion, her message was obvious.

Critics of ape intelligence studies dismiss anecdotes such as these, and argue that the trainers are reading meaningfulness into the animal's responses. For example, both Sebeok and H. S. Terrace of Columbia University, who have been studying chimpanzees' communication skills for several years, argue that these anecdotes were only accidentally meaningful. Terrace believes that when asked about the swan, Washoe probably didn't know if her trainer was asking her to identify the bird or the lake. She therefore may have signed correctly for both (i.e., "water" and then "bird") and the trainer linked the two signs together. Terrace has a similar explanation for the "dirty Roger" incident. Washoe had been taught to sign "dirty" when she had to be taken to the toilet. The use of the word may have become associated in the chimp's mind with a desire to be removed from her present location, no matter what the context. The term "dirty Roger" may have been Washoe's manipulative attempt to get Roger to take her for a walk (remove her from her present environment);

it may not have been the direct pejorative the trainer interpreted.

Dr. Terrace concluded by making one of the strongest presentations of the conference. He gave, in fact, a mini-history of his own attempts to study chimpanzee language skills and his journey from enthusiasm to utter discouragement.

Dr. Terrace began his work in 1973 by teaching a male chimp called Nim Chimpsky to communicate in sign language. The chimp had been born at the Oklahoma Institute for Primate Study, and eventually was shipped to New York, where Terrace studied him in his lab at Columbia University. Nim soon had a staggering vocabulary and eventually began to string words together in astounding ways. He even seemed to be developing a simple grammar. Terrace initially believed that Nim was learning communication skills in the same way a child learns to use language. Over a two-year period, more than 2,000 of Nim's "utterances" were recorded. Typical of these were such explicit phrases as "more hug," "want more drink," etc. Eventually the Columbia psychologist and his associates began videotaping Nim's signings—and that's when disillusionment set in.

It gradually dawned on Terrace that while Nim was indeed stringing together words, he did not seem to be learning a communication skill in the manner of a child acquiring language. The first clue came when Terrace realized that while Nim was learning more and more words, his sentences were not growing appreciably longer. Children normally lengthen their phrases as they acquire language skill, and also often speak spontaneously as they learn to use language, but not the chimps, the psychologist realized. Videotapes of Nim's learning sessions showed that the chimp had to be cajoled into making sign language responses. He didn't volunteer phrases. Also, in a way quite different from children who in early childhood listen to their parents before they speak, Nim freely interrupted his mentor, showing little attempt to communicate with him in a meaningful way.

Dr. Terrace's hopes that chimps could be trained to develop a crude language and thus communicate with humans sank to an all-time low when he began to review his videotapes, at which point he discovered that Nim's trainers often actually cued (shades of Clever Hans!) appropriate responses from the chimp. For instance, once Nim was shown a cat by his trainer Susan Quimby and he signed, "me hug cat." This seemed an intelligent and appropriate response—but photographs of the session revealed that Nim had actually been directed to make this response. The trainer had been signing "you" when the chimp signed "me" and "who" when Nim responded with "cat." These were appropriate responses Nim had learned by rote, and the trainer had intentionally cued the chimp to give a meaningful response to the presence of the cat.

With evidence like this on hand, one might have thought the the world of ape communication had suffered an irreversible setback, but Duane and Sue Savage-Rumbaugh were ready for such criticisms and presented the conference with startling evidence of their own. The Rumbaughs have been training several other chimps besides Lana, around whom their work originally focused. They are currently videotaping sessions in which two communicating apes are placed in a "playpen" environment completely isolated from human observers. They are finding that even when lab workers are not present the chimps often seem to be teaching signs to each other!

The Rumbaughs' view—that chimps are capable of developing true communication skills—has been supported by some new findings made by Dr. Suzanne Chevalier-Skolnikoff of Stanford University. She too has been studying the spontaneous word linkages composed by apes trained in signing. Dr. Chevalier-Skolnikoff argued before the Academy that apes do not seem to be merely reciting conditioned responses when "communicating" with their trainers, but seem to be developing cognition as well. She first came to this conclusion when she noted that chimps, when annoyed, often will foul up their trainers by giving humorous or deceitful responses to questions. The use of humor or deceit can be employed only when (for instance) a child truly understands what he is trying to communicate. Simple cuing, argued Dr. Chevalier-Skolnikoff, cannot account for this highly evolved method of communication. The fact that "talking" chimps do communicate in this way indicates that they are not only learning vocabulary through sign language and other communication methods, but are also learning how to use their skills.

The debate over animal communications is bound to go on. I left the New York Academy of Science's conference more confused than ever. It was difficult to tell whether Sebeok or the Rumbaughs had made the stronger case.

But it shouldn't be thought that the New York Academy's conference had no positive outcomes. Prof.

Heini Hediger, an esteemed authority on animal behavior from the University of Zurich, had begun the conference by stating that if chimps could develop communication skills, the day might come when animal psychologists could convince them to clean up their own cages and scrub the floors.

Dr. Rumbaugh was quick to point out that his chimps at Emory University had been trained to do just that! And, he added, that was more than his graduate students could be trained to do.

Animals and Life After Death

We human beings, who are the crown of creation, are the only creatures aware of our own existence because only we possess souls. And of course since only we possess souls, only we will survive bodily death. How little we know ...

Are Cats Immortal?

Paul M. Vest
June 1955

Do you ever watch a cat and wonder what mystic secrets lie behind his strange, disturbing eyes; eyes which seem always to look through and beyond you?

Are you ever a bit irritated by the cat's air of superiority; his obvious disinterest in you?

I do and am. Therefore I admit frankly that cats were never my favorite animals. In fact, I'd always considered them cold, indifferent, and inordinately selfish creatures until I had the following experiences, which made me wonder if a cat might not have good reason for behaving like a superior being.

The first experience occurred some years ago when I moved to a house in the Wilshire district in Los Angeles. One of my neighbors was a friendly, motherly woman in her early 70s. Her name was Mrs. Martha Rovello. As we became well acquainted, she visited me frequently with a plate of freshly baked cookies or a homemade pie.

One morning, as I walked into her yard, I noticed a large white angora cat dozing in the sun on the porch. As I approached, it got up lazily, stretched itself and ambled away. I noticed odd black markings on its hind legs.

Later, while talking to Mrs. Rovello, I casually mentioned her big white cat. She looked at me oddly and exclaimed, "But I haven't a cat now!"

"Then it was probably just a stray on your porch," I replied.

She was looking at me intently. "It was a white cat?" she persisted. "Could it have been an angora?"

I described the cat and mentioned the odd black markings on its hind legs.

She stared at me incredulously. "Why that's Whitey!" she exclaimed excitedly. "But it couldn't be. Whitey was killed almost a year ago!"

She got up nervously, and insisted that we go out and search the yard for the cat. We looked high and low, but the cat was nowhere to be seen.

I was completely mystified. She declared that I had given an exact description of her Whitey—but Whitey had been dead for months!

Later, I decided that I must have seen a stray cat which resembled Whitey and let it go at that. I'd practically forgotten the incident when, one afternoon about six months later, I chanced to glance over into Mrs. Rovello's yard. Without paying much attention at first, I noticed two cats playing in the grass. One was a gray calico cat, and the other was a white cat with black markings on its hind legs. I felt a tremor of excitement as I suddenly realized that the white cat was the one Mrs. Rovello had believed was her Whitey.

I watched the two cats for a moment, and then ran over to the fence to get a better view. As though startled, the white cat turned and looked at me and then it was no longer there! Only the calico cat remained—apparently shadow boxing with itself. An odd feeling passed over me. I stood staring at the grey cat as it continued to play with an invisible companion. Obviously, from the actions of the grey cat, Whitey was still playing too, only I could no longer see him.

I pondered that experience for days. I tried to figure it from every angle, but I always came up with the same answer. As fantastic as it seemed, I must have seen the "ghost" or astral body of Whitey—a cat killed months before. Apparently, Whitey was living in some ordinarily invisible dimension within the boundaries of his former home. Also, it seemed evident that the calico cat could see Whitey and play with him as easily as though Whitey were still in his physical body.

The more I thought about Whitey, the more puzzled I became. Finally, I persuaded a friend who had several cats to let me have one of them—a jet black animal named Jezebel. Jezebel was not a friendly cat. I pampered her with cream and choice tidbits, but from the first nothing influenced that cat's regard for me. She remained proud, haughty, and disdainful toward me. Possibly with her feline intelligence she understood that I wanted her solely for experimental purposes. I was anxious to observe her reactions to the "ghost" cat who lived next door.

I'll never forget the afternoon I took her over to Mrs. Rovello's yard and put her down. She picked her way disinterestedly about, sniffed delicately at a bed of nasturtiums. She made a few passes at a bright-winged butterfly. Nothing unusual happened until she started to go onto the porch. She froze on the steps, hissing and baring her fangs. She was staring wild-eyed at the identical spot on the porch where I first saw the white cat dozing in the sun.

Mrs. Rovello came running out onto the porch and exclaimed, "What on earth's wrong with that cat?"

"Apparently Whitey and Jezebel aren't kindred souls," I answered with an attempt at humor I didn't feel.

Mrs. Rovello stared at the cat and then at me. "Do you think that cat sees ... sees Whitey?" she asked nervously.

"Well it's certain she sees something," I replied feeling pretty uncomfortable. "And that is the same spot where I once thought I saw Whitey ..."

As we both stared at the strange antics of the black cat, she turned swiftly and bolted for home.

Mrs. Rovello shook her head and with a nervous tremor in her voice she said, "You know that's real strange, but Whitey never did like black cats. It sort of gives a body the creeps."

I never could get Jezebel back into Mrs. Rovello's yard, and as she became more irascible daily, I thankfully returned her to her original owner.

My strange experiences with the ghost of Whitey continued to puzzle me. As a result, I did a considerable amount of research on the subject of cats. I learned that ancient people held them in awe and frequently worshiped them. In many civilizations, they have been cryptic symbols of the occult, the mysterious, and the unknown. Oriental priests believed them to be clairvoyant and clairaudient, able to see both the past and future as easily as we view the present. In the Middle Ages, cats were believed to accompany witches to the rites of the Witches Sabbat. Also, necromancers and magicians have always employed cats in the practice of their secret arts.

Of course, all of this is considered the rankest superstition in these enlightened days, but following my strange experiences with Whitey I occasionally wonder if the ancients had been wiser about some things than we are today, with all of our materialistic advancements.

At any rate, I never saw the "ghost" of Whitey again, and when I moved to another neighborhood my interest in cats dwindled, for it seemed a mystery I could never solve, but my most profound mystic experience with a cat was yet to come.

Some years later my friends, the Carl Andersons, in Beverly Hills, had a beautiful, tawny Persian cat named Tiger. Tiger was unusually friendly, and apparently took a great liking to me. Whenever I visited the Andersons, Tiger always came bounding out to meet me, and when I sat down he jumped into my lap and commenced purring.

In fact, Tiger, through some extra-sensory perceptive ability, even seemed to know when I was coming to the house. The Andersons told me that frequently, five or ten minutes before I was due to arrive, Tiger would beg to be let out. Later, when I drove up, he would be at the gate waiting for me.

Then occurred the most incredible of all my experiences with cats. It happened late one afternoon when I entered the Anderson's yard. My mind was preoccupied with some personal troubles, but I wondered why Tiger wasn't at the gate to meet me. Then I saw him, sound asleep in a patch of sunlight beneath an avocado tree. The instant I noticed him, a startling, incredible thing happened—immediately above Tiger and within some sort of inner depthness, Tiger's double appeared, fully awake, vibrant with life, and looking directly at me. In fact the "double" appeared much more vividly alive and infinitely more beautiful than the physical Tiger ever had. I was literally dumfounded as I stood there transfixed, doubting my senses.

Perhaps the entire experience lasted no longer than sixty seconds, but in that minute I seemed intuitively to know that cats are really immortal and consciously aware of their immortality. In other words, I understood then that cats are able to project their astral bodies at will and are as conscious in higher vibratory dimensions as we are in the physical world.

Oh, I have since doubted that experience. I have called myself a superstitious idiot. I have tried to convince myself that it was only some sort of optical illusion, but I still wonder—did I stumble upon the ancient mystery of the cat?

I ask myself, "Could the priests of the ancient wisdom-religions have been right? Could they with their spiritual vision actually see the conscious, astral projection of cats? Were they correct in their belief that the cat is the most mystical of creatures and lives mysteriously in that borderland region between the physical world and higher dimensions?"

Despite my experiences, I tell myself that such thinking is superstition. Yet whenever I see a cat regarding me with secret, sphinx-like eyes, I wonder what he really sees. Does he view human beings imprisoned in bodies of death, unable consciously to leave their physical tombs, and feel only disdain for such pathetic creatures. Of course, I tell myself, it's all the wildest fancy ... and yet ... I wonder.

My Beloved Ghosts

Wilman Thone
February 1967

Five-year-old Dan, a great dappled gelding, and Beauty, a coal-black mare a year younger, were friends. Their attachment for each other provoked the horse-breeder who raised them because they refused to work with proper harness-mates—horses of the same color. They would work only together. Their recalcitrance broke up two matched teams for the breeder, and for this reason he sold them to us at a quite reasonable price.

We acquired our Ohio farm in January, 1936, and bought Dan and Beauty in February. In late May, Beauty gave birth to a tiny mare, a carbon copy of her own delightful self. We named the foal Little Meg, and soon came to idolize her. She had the freedom of the farm, roaming at will as if she were a cat or dog. She picked her way through the garden, following the paths and never trampling a single plant. She worked in harness too and equally well with Dan or Beauty. Sometimes she was put in the traces as a third horse—mostly just to please her because she would trot along anyhow.

Little Meg had amusing ways. In warm weather she often stood with her head hanging over the porch railing, where she could look into the house and watch us. When she wanted water (the watering-tub was made from a barrel cut in half), she always put one foot in the tub and stirred and stirred until the water was well roiled—then she drank. Sometimes, if her feet were muddy, her "soup" would become unpalatable and she wouldn't drink it. She would step on the edge of the tub to tip it and drain the contents and then neigh for someone to pump more water for her.

When she became ill in January 1941, Little Meg was almost five. At first we thought she had only a cold, but she quickly grew worse and died. We were broken-hearted, but the horses didn't seem to know she was gone. Dan's stall was first in line, then Meg's, then Beauty's—and neither of the older horses would enter Meg's stall. They behaved as if a horse already occupied the stall.

When Meg was alive, she often teased Beauty by standing in her way. Beauty would nudge her and make a sound like "huff, huff, huff," until Meg stepped up. Other times Meg would lie down in Beauty's path and the older horse had to wait for her to get up so that she could pass. After Meg died, Beauty continued to go through these motions, much to my bewilderment.

Other occurrences were more noticeable. For instance, the man who sold us the horses witnessed the activity around the watering-tub. While we stood watching, the water would roil just as it had when Meg stirred it. The team always waited until the water quieted. Other times when Dan and Beauty were drinking with their heads close together, something seemed to push between them—just as Meg always had. Beauty would step back, making a welcoming "huff, huff" sound, while another nose seemed to find its way into the tub.

In hot weather the horses were put to pasture at dusk and brought in during the heat of the day. One morning the sky was overcast and the horses were left in the pasture until the sun came out. When it grew hot

I went to call them in, and to my astonishment I saw Little Meg quietly grazing with the other two. I ran toward her, calling her name—and she disappeared. Then I thought my imagination was working overtime, but as time went by I often saw her in the field at night. However, I could get just so close, and then she was gone. Once she raised her head and turned her melting brown eyes toward me before she vanished.

Horses must be kept inside during the winter, for to slip on the frozen ground and break a leg brings their end. In the spring of 1948, when he did get out, Dan was full of ginger. He raced round and round the pasture, then stood kicking in sheer exuberance. But suddenly he groaned and lay down. Dan never did this; he even slept standing. We managed to get him to his feet and into his stall where he fell again. The vet could do nothing. Dan lingered two days, then left us.

It was raining softly the night Dan died. We had no electricity then, but a lantern dimly lighted the stable door. Inside the stable, the men waited to see if Dan's condition would change. Beauty stood at the porch, her head over the rail in Meg's old position. I was talking to Beauty when I heard it—the shrill wild neigh that could come only from the throat of Meg. Beauty's ears twitched and she looked back at the barn—as I did. There in the glow of the lantern stood Little Meg.

In the twinkling of an eye Dan stood beside her. They whirled and galloped off into the night. I listened to their fading hoofbeats and knew I had not imagined it.

A few minutes later the men came in. "Dan just died," one of them said. "He died just as the horse called. Must be in a pasture nearby if it wasn't Beauty here."

I knew it wasn't Beauty. Of course there were horses in neighboring pastures, but when you live with animals you know their voices. I knew it was Meg's voice we had heard.

After Dan's death, I never again saw Meg in the pasture—although Beauty didn't seem lonely. She would enter any stall, but she still preferred her own. Then we bought another gelding to make up a team, a young fellow named Tony. The team worked well and the next six years were uneventful.

In 1954, when Beauty died, she was about twenty years old. It was August and very warm. When I put the horses out that night, Beauty limped a little and before leaving me at the gate she rubbed her soft nose against my shoulder. At the time I didn't think much of it, because she always was affectionate and liked to be petted. Later I remembered and wondered if perhaps she was saying good-bye.

Something awakened me about 2:30 A.M. I thought I had heard a horse call. Thinking Beauty wanted to get in because a light rain had started, I listened for another call. It didn't come, so slipping into boots and a raincoat I hurried out to the barnyard.

By this time we had electric power and the yard lights made the barnyard as bright as day. Beauty, I knew, would be standing at the south gate, with the cows on the other side of the fence and Tony somewhere nearby. I hurried around the end of the barn— and stopped dead in my tracks.

There in the light, in the slanting warm rain, stood Little Meg, plainly silhouetted against the lighter, larger shape of Dan. Both were looking at the south gate, which was out of my line of vision. Meg threw up her head, tossed it in the old familiar way, and gave the rousing welcoming neigh I knew so well. Suddenly Beauty appeared at her side and the three horses whirled and disappeared into the darkness.

I switched on more lights and walked through the cowshed. Beauty's body, warm but lifeless, lay in a mud puddle. Sadly, I threw a tarp over her and looked up to see Tony and the cows watching me. Did they too see inside the gates of Hereafter?

Now Tony was allowed the freedom of the box stall, and became as great a pet as Little Meg and the others. With farming heartlessly mechanized, we had no need for another horse and it took all my powers of persuasion to keep the head of the house from selling Tony. Often I wondered, "Will the 'gang' come back for Tony when it is his time to go?"

I never shall forget the hot, fly-ridden summer of 1959, the year Tony took sick. I had been giving him a tonic for some time. I lathered his back and sides to keep off the flies, and put netting over his ears and eyes. One day he staggered weakly as if he were drugged. I barely could lead him into the barn without getting stepped on. I turned him into the box stall and started the car to go to the next farm to telephone the veterinarian. When Tony heard the car start, he went frantic. I went back to quiet him, but again, at the noise of the car starting, he thrashed around as if he couldn't bear to be alone. I left the car where he could see it and went on foot to the telephone.

The vet was out, but his wife said she'd send him to us as soon as he returned. I went back to the barn to find Tony nervously pacing. When he leaned against the stall as if resting I walked out to the end of the barnyard to watch for the vet. From where I stood I could see the curving drive that led to the stable door and Tony's head through the open half-door of his stall.

As I waited I became aware of a dim drumming sound, a throbbing that slowly but steadily came nearer. Tony raised his head, moving nervously. The sound deepened. In the three-quarter mile lane separating the farm from the main road, a cloud of dust formed. It came closer as the sound increased—then swept past me, rounding the curve to the stable door. The rush of air fluttered my sleeve and the warm smell of horses enveloped me. Tony reared and his head disappeared from sight as he crashed to the floor. Then Little Meg's joyous triumphant call rang out on the sunny air.

I held my breath. At the stable door the foggy shapes stirred and became three horses, my beloved horses! The door opened smartly and Tony came out. He was just a misty shape, but it was Tony—just as the others were Beauty, Dan, and Little Meg.

Together they started their return trip to Forever. Stepping into the lane, right into their path, I opened my arms wide and called them by name. They rushed at me and again a warm rich-smelling mist closed over me. I felt a soft nose nuzzle my cheek in passing. Then they were gone and the sound was fading.

A new cloud of dust heralded the approach of the vet.

"Tony just left," I said tonelessly. He nodded and drove on to the barn.

When the Lord stretches out His Hand to me, will Meg bring the "gang" to escort me over the line? Will I hear her call once more?

The Kitten Came for Phil

Alice Morgan
September 1980

My brother, Phil D'Amico, was eight and one-half years old when he died of leukemia on July 11, 1966. He had suffered the ravages of the disease with incredible bravery and maturity, and often expressed his innocent, deeply moving faith that he would continue to live after death.

His third-grade classmates, in an attempt to bring him some pleasure, took up a collection to buy Phil a darling little orange Persian kitten, but the gift came too late. The kitten arrived as we returned to our Yonkers, New York, home after having laid little Phil to rest.

Our parents, exhausted and grief-stricken, were not keen on having a pet, and asked the pet shop delivery man to take the kitten back, explaining that Phil had passed on. The man was holding the kitten in his arms when suddenly it squirmed loose, jumped to the floor, and dashed wildly up the stairs to the second-floor. With a hurried apology the man rushed after the cat. In what had been Phil's room, he cornered the animal. The kitten was crouched at the head of the bed, claws firmly anchored in Phil's pillow. When my parents saw the pleading look in the kitten's eyes, they couldn't resist; they agreed to keep him after all.

We called him Phil's Kitty, which after a while was shortened to Skitty, and the little animal took his place as a family member in no time at all. Somehow he seemed like Phil, extremely affectionate and gently playful. As the months passed, we could not fail to notice there was something quite unusual about Skitty and although we did not often talk about it, we all came to suspect that Phil was trying to communicate with us through the kitten.

Skitty insisted on sleeping in Phil's now empty room, and repeated attempts to lock him out brought forth endless pitiful wailing. At 3:15 each afternoon, the time when Phil would have come home from school, the kitten appeared in the kitchen to beg for a snack. It had been Phil's habit to have milk and cookies every afternoon at that very hour.

The truly incredible event that turned our suspicions into unshakable belief occurred the following November, on the day that would have been Phil's ninth birthday. Skitty was now about seven or eight months old. On that day Skitty suddenly appeared in the front yard of the Mallory house. Jimmy Mallory had been Phil's best friend. The cat was rolling Phil's pink rubber ball along with his little furry paws. Jimmy's home was a full two blocks away. How the cat traversed that distance, dodging traffic and maneuvering the ball up and down curbs, was beyond our comprehension. And how could he have known Jimmy's house?

Jimmy's mother had been raking leaves in the front yard when she spotted Skitty. Knowing that he never strayed from our yard, she called us immediately. We were stunned, for we hadn't even noticed that Skitty was missing. The cat had been playing with Phil's ball under our oak tree—but now he seemed to be indicating that Jimmy was to have the ball. What better way to celebrate Phil's birthday?

Other incidents through the years reaffirmed our belief that Phil was indeed "alive" and speaking to us through Skitty. In May 1974, the cat, now eight years old, started to lose weight. The vet diagnosed feline lymphosarcoma—a fatal disease similar to the one that took Phil. There was no cure, no treatment. We tried to make Skitty's last days as comfortable as possible and like Phil, the cat tolerated the illness with dignity. He purred when he was stroked up until the day he died— July 11, 1974, eight years to the day after Phil's death.

Later that year I married John Morgan and moved to my own home in a nearby town. I had developed a deep admiration and love for cats, but we did not have one because my husband is allergic to cat dander. One evening the following summer, I awoke in the middle of the night to the sound of a cat leaping onto my bed. There is an odd half-muffled "mrrr" that cats "say" as they land after leaping; it is an unmistakable sound. I was startled, but didn't want to wake my husband. I reached out in the darkness and felt a long-haired cat about the size and fluffiness of Skitty. I felt for the ears. One had a V-shaped notch, just as Skitty had had. It was incredible!

My husband, apparently awakened by my movements and sharp intake of breath, sat up and switched on the light. As he did so, the feeling of a cat under my hand vanished. I told him what had happened but he passed it off as a dream. I knew it wasn't a dream but I didn't argue.

The next morning as I was making the bed I found several orange-buff cat hairs on my pillow, exactly the color of Skitty's fur. There had been a cat in my bedroom the night before. I looked at the calendar. The date was July 11, 1975.

Guardian Dog, Guardian Angel

D. Roger Martin
May 1980

Was Rusti just a marvelous companion dog or something more? A guardian angel, perhaps?

Rusti stared up at Rhonda Marshall, an elderly woman for whom I was doing some carpentry. My dog always watched strangers and friends alike.

"You are indeed fortunate," Mrs. Marshall said.

"Yes, Rusti's a beautiful animal."

"More than that. This animal is your life. She is your guardian."

Suddenly uncomfortable, I tried to shrug off her words. I said, "Dogs are faithful. They're known as protectors."

The woman's gaze drifted from mine to lock with Rusti's.

"But there is a great difference between mere blind loyalty and direct purpose. It is this animal's purpose in life to see that you survive. She is your guardian."

That conversation took place in the summer of 1968. Richard Nixon was running for President again. Carl Yastrzemski would capture his third batting title with a record low .301 batting average. Rusti was barely a year old and I was approaching my twenty-third birthday. The old woman's words gave me a chill, for Rusti had already saved my life twice.

On two occasions, faulty oil stoves started fires in my apartment. In both cases, Rusti licked my face until I woke up—although I was half-drugged by fumes. These events were only the beginning of a chain of events to follow, and the old woman's words often would return to me.

Rusti was half Brittany spaniel and half fox terrier and I got her when she was about four months old. By her second year of life she had attained a weight of thirty-eight pounds. Aside from a week I spent in the hospital when she lost five pounds, and while she was pregnant when she gained six, thirty-eight pounds was her standard weight. Her face was sharp-featured, her attentive amber eyes radiated intelligence, and her ears were constantly alert. If she lowered her head and tail simultaneously, it meant a stranger had betrayed something to her deep awareness. The stranger would do well to become scarce immediately.

A strange communication developed between us. For instance, if I watched TV, Rusti would curl up in a chair next to me. I could rise wordlessly a dozen times to switch channels or to make a sandwich and she wouldn't stir, but when I thought, "I might as well take Rusti for a walk," she would bound out of the chair ready to go. My acquaintances usually loved her, but her constant vigil made some of them a trifle nervous, and many were decidedly unnerved by her eyes, which glowed like red coals at night.

During the day Rusti played in the river or the winter snow. At night, I walked her for an hour or more. We fished together, worked together, lived together. It was a great life. Or was it?

Soon after the second fire incident, my marriage collapsed and I undertook a long bout with alcohol. Many times I had no idea how I got home, but Rusti was always nearby. One time, two teenagers found me passed out. They told me the next day that Rusti had been pacing around my fallen form like a sentinel.

"And," they added, " she wasn't exactly receiving callers."

Then, late in 1969, my ex-wife was killed—murdered, to be precise. Murder is something you read about every day, but it never happens in your life. Well, it happened in mine. In fact, I was an early suspect and was picked up for questioning. Luckily for me, the guilty parties were soon apprehended.

Still, living in a small Vermont community has certain disadvantages. Much of the blame for my wife's tragic death fell on my shoulders—although she had been involved with a drug dealer who wanted to chuck the racket for her sake. It isn't that easy to break from a drug ring, and it cost them both their lives. Nevertheless, my life was in shambles. My sole consolation was a red and white mongrel with a crooked stripe between her eyes, who greeted me as if I were the most important human being in the world. Often I thought of old Mrs. Marshall's words.

A year passed, and I was in love and headed for my second marriage. In March 1971, my new wife Mary and I watched with delight as Rusti gave birth to five black and white puppies (half-black Labrador retriever). One of the puppies was named Ralph, and remained in our lives as my parents' pet. When our son David and later our daughter Donna were born, everything seemed to be working to perfection. Even the Red Sox got into the 1975 World Series.

But by May 1976, my second marriage had ended and I embarked on the worst two years of my life. Suicide was prominent in my thoughts; at times I thought it was the only relief available.

As if she were reading my thoughts, Rusti would sense my despair, climb into my lap, and shiver or whine. That would set me thinking. Who would take care of Rusti? Who would give her bones and chewies, and take her on trips to the river? I knew the answer. No one. Rusti needed me. Perhaps that isn't a lot by some standards, but it was enough. Rusti needed me. Again the old woman's words crossed my mind.

In 1976 I turned my hand to writing, and it was all uphill from there, but together Rusti and I made it all the way into 1980. She was featured in many of the poems and short stories that I published, and gradually we took on life, one round at a time. We won a few, lost a few, but always gave a good account of ourselves.

Then on March 28, 1980, Rusti died.

The next day, in a sleeting rain, I buried my oldest and dearest friend near the Third Branch River she had loved so much. It seemed like the proper place.

Life was terribly empty without Rusti. During that summer I went fishing exactly twice. It just wasn't the same without Rusti playing on the bank or splashing in the river.

On the sixth of August (I marked it on my calendar), I saw Rusti again. I had taken my parents' dog, Ralph, for a walk about midnight, and we had just crossed the footbridge over the river on our way home. Ralph began to wag his tail—and I saw something beneath the pines, waiting. I feared it might be a skunk and took in the slack of Ralph's leash, but Ralph wasn't straining hard. He was simply wagging his tail as he would when greeting a friend. As we drew nearer the waiting figure, I could make out white markings and sufficient size to derail any thoughts of a prowling skunk. It occurred to me that an old bird dog lived nearby; probably it was he. I let Ralph have the slack again and we strolled into the heavy shadows beneath the pines, now certain it was the friendly old bird dog. I could make out a light-colored nose reaching forward to greet Ralph.

"How you doing, old boy?" I asked leaning over to scratch the old dog's head.

The head lifted and the dog looked straight at me, eyes shining red like two coals in the dark. I saw Rusti's crooked white stripe and her wagging tail. If hair can stand on end from fright, mine did. I stood transfixed, staring down into Rusti's unmistakable face. Suddenly, as if pulled by some unseen power, she was swept in a wide circle away from us toward the footbridge. I lost sight of her—but it didn't matter. Her grave was only a dozen yards from the footbridge. She was going back.

Was this Rusti's last message? She had helped to show me life was okay and was she now showing me that the other side is okay too?

It's as if she said, "See? I'm okay. Hang in there, kid."

And you can bet I'll do just that. Rusti has worked hard to get me this far.

"She is your guardian," old Mrs. Marshall had said.

Even after death.

Dog's Love Conquers Death

Gail P. Shevitz
April 1975

Late in the afternoon of November 27, 1973, I stopped at Happy Harry's Pharmacy in Brookside, Delaware, where my husband Harold worked, to tell him my shopping was done and I was going home. The look he turned to me made my heart stop.

"What is it?" I whispered.

He hesitated, then blurted out, "Woody Gonce called, hon, and said that Mynyak has been hit by a car."

He didn't have to tell me the beautiful Afghan hound I loved so much was dead; I knew by the look in his eyes. All the way home, I kept hearing my husband's voice repeating what our neighbor had told him: in the heavy fog Mynyak had been hit and was lying beside the road. I felt my heart would break. I had to find him and take him home.

I knew I shouldn't try to do it alone, but I had to. As I came abreast of the Gonce farm, I slowed the car. Mynyak was supposed to be between Woody's house and ours. Keeping the car at a crawl I looked from one side of the road to the other until through a break in the fog I saw our mailbox. I had gone the distance from Woody's place to ours, but somehow had passed Mynyak. I backed the car and began again. After driving up and down for about twenty minutes, I gave up and parked the car at the side of the road. Armed with a flahlight I searched again, this time on foot, although in the swirling fog I could hardly see the road under my feet, much less the shoulder where Mynyak was sure to be.

I seemed to have walked for hours when headlights shone dimly through the fog. It was my husband and together we began again the grisly search—but to no avail. We couldn't find Mynyak. My heart took hope; perhaps he wasn't dead, but that hope died when Woody came out to help, for he had seen the dog hit. Where, then, was his body?

Nearly exhausted, I stood on our front porch wrapped in a blanket and watched the eerie lights of a third search bobbing up and down. Finally I couldn't stand being alone and plodded over to the stable. A tear trickled down my cold cheek as I stroked the old mare's nose and she nuzzled me in response. Except for the soft sounds of the other horses rummaging in their stalls, everything was quiet. Then, suddenly, a pitiful cry of fear rent the silent night.

Sudden sweat beaded my forehead; I stood rigid with fear. I turned woodenly toward the stable door, and there in a shroud of fog stood Mynyak! Nothing could equal the joy I felt as I reached out to clutch him to me, but he eluded me and as if in slow motion began to run.

"Mynyak," I cried, "come back!" But he was loping away, so I followed. We had gone some distance into the woods behind the house when Mynyak disappeared into a thicket.

I tried to hurry after him, clutching at the under-brush to keep my footing in the fog-shrouded woods. I tripped and fell, then came feebly to my knees. I looked in vain for Mynyak, whispering his name over and over. Then miraculously the fog parted and Mynyak was in front of me again, staring with conscience-stricken eyes, as if he knew the agony I felt, but had a reason for leading me on.

For what seemed miles we kept on into the dense woods, my weary, bruised body complaining at every step of the blind, incredibly slow pursuit. Finally, we came to what seemed to be a clearing. I heard strange guttural, frightening sounds and I saw Mynyak bare his teeth. He had a terrible look. Then, in one awful moment, my eyes took in a horrible sight. At last I knew why Mynyak had brought me here.

Torn and bleeding, our sweet little goat "Sugar," Mynyak's lifetime companion, huddled against some rocks with a look of sick fear in her eyes. Beside her was the baby she had miraculously just borne and by the look of her torn body had fought long and hard to save from two hungry wild dogs now feasting on the other kid Sugar had not been able to save.

As I took in the awful scene, I became an animal myself. Dazed as I was, my mind began to work quickly and coldly as I watched the two wild dogs. They looked at me contemptuously, their glowing yellow eyes terrible to see. They began to move toward me. Terrible fear and rage possessed me as the dogs lurched sickeningly through the air. Before I knew I had moved, they were scrambling beneath the blanket I had thrown over them, the blanket that incredibly I had not lost in my long pursuit of Mynyak. In a flash I was blindly beating the blanket with a heavy branch I didn't even remember picking up.

Aghast, I realized the thing I was beating was no longer moving and the other dog had run off long since. I stared at the grotesque form under the blanket, and waves of nausea rolled over me. I dropped to the ground.

When I recovered, I called Sugar's name. She moved slowly toward me on shaky legs. I picked up her frail baby and my eyes filled as I watched Sugar look at the pitiful torn body of her other baby. Her large eyes wavered, closed ever so slightly, then she came to me. I called softly to Mynyak to follow, but I knew in my heart he would not come. He lay quietly, a look of sadness in his eyes.

I felt humble as the fog slowly began to lift, and a glorious moon shone through to light our way. Barely comprehending what had happened, I set my mind to getting Sugar and her baby home. When I came out of the woods holding my tender burden, my husband was waiting for me.

"We found him," he said, "about twenty minutes ago, but hon, he wasn't there before, I know he wasn't.

They had found Mynyak's body at about the same time I had seen him for the last time. Mynyak was dead, but some part of him stayed long enough to save the friend he loved so much. In our hearts and memories he will always live.

When I watch Sugar's baby "Spice" leaping freely and joyfully in the green grass, I gaze at the sky and whisper, "Thank you, Mynyak."

Mystery Animals

Cryptozoology is a new science dedicated to the study of "hidden animals"—animals whose existence is attested to in anecdotal reports, but for which firm physical evidence is lacking. Such an animal is the Nandi bear. In other cases, the animal's existence, at least at one time, is not in dispute. The Tasmanian tiger, for example, officially became extinct in 1936—but alleged sightings of this strange animal have continued ever since, pitting skeptical wildlife biologists against a growing number of witnesses who claim brief, tantalizing encounters with it in the wild.

Is There a Nandi Bear?

Willy Ley
July 1963

Leafing through the very useful, one-volume natural history book entitled *World Natural History*, by E. G. Boulenger, director of the aquarium of the Zoological Society of London, I came across the following remarks:

"Some twenty years ago (which is to say about 1920), weird stories were widely circulated in our press concerning a strange animal known as the Nandi bear, frequenting Kenya Colony, and peculiarly given to attacking women and children. The stories became so persistent that the British Museum authorities instituted an enquiry.

"As a result, skins and skulls of the alleged bear were sent to England. These were always those of either leopards or hyenas, the skull of one often being forwarded with the skin of the other—the two being alleged to belong to one and the same animal. Finally, a tracing of the 'bear's' footprint arrived. This showed six toes, a state of things unknown amongst mammals recent or extinct. Close examination showed it to be two impressions of hyena pads, one superimposed upon the other, and so the legend of the 'Nandi bear' was at last dispelled ..."

While I have no doubt that the British Museum received shipments of leopard and hyena skin and skulls in all possible combinations, and while I wonder what kind of a person could manage to live in Africa and know so little about wildlife that he did not become suspicious when confronted with a six-toed footprint, I have to say that the case is not quite as simple as it has been made out by Professor Boulenger.

To begin at the most fundamental level, Africa is one of the few places left on earth where a fairly large animal might still exist without being known to science. During the years from 1900 to 1914, not less than three large mammals were discovered there. It began in 1900, when Sir Harry Johnston discovered the short-necked giraffe, now generally known as the okapi.

The streak of discoveries continued when, in 1904, Captain Meinertzhagen of the British East African Rifles discovered an unknown species of wild pigs in the Ituri Forest, named, in his honor, *Hylochoerus meinertzhageni*.

The discoveries reached a third climax when the German explorer and animal hunter Hans Schomburgk discovered, in 1911, an animal which had been believed to be extinct. It had been described by natives and missionaries as an enormous black pig which was very dangerous, but the officials of Liberia stated with visible relief that it no longer existed in Liberia; "if it ever lived in our country," they added.

The "enormous black pig" not only existed, it turned out to be identical with an animal described by the American physician Dr. Samuel Morton in 1844. But Dr. Morton had not seen the animal, he only had a skull to go by and had concluded, from the study of that skull, that it had belonged to a relative of the hippopotamus. The animal found by Schomburgk was what is now called the pygmy hippopotamus.

More discoveries were to be made. In 1937, Dr. James Chapin of New York discovered the bird *Afropavo congensis,* the Congo peacock.

It is only natural that a man like Hans Schomburgk, with one major discovery to his credit, looked around for more. I listened to him in 1930 in Berlin, at the occasion of a privately arranged small lecture which he devoted to rumors he had heard. There were rumors of a dangerous animal living in the inland swamps, rivers, and lakes, which went under a name which would translate as "water elephant." There were rumors about a pygmy rhinoceros which was supposed to live somewhere in the mountains.

And there was a story about an animal called *Too,* which was said to be all black, to have a "very bad face," and which sometimes attacked without the least provocation. When somebody asked Schomburgk which of these stories he believed, he said that he had been shown a piece of skin covered with reddish-brown hair that was said to have come from the "water elephant." But he added that his mention of this piece of skin was not meant to imply that he did not think the stories of the pygmy rhinoceros and the Too were just stories.

The first point in favor of the existence of the Nandi bear that could be brought up by its defenders is what has just been mentioned: namely that Africa is just the place where additional discoveries are possible, even likely.

The second point in defense of the Nandi bear is somewhat more sophisticated. This point is that it is very strange there are no bears in Africa. The bear tribe is well-represented everywhere else, except, of course, on the two isolated continents of Australia and Antarctica.

Here in the United States we have *Ursus americanus*, the well-known black bear and the not quite as well known *Ursus ornatus*, the spectacled bear. And we have last, but by no means least, *Ursus horribilis*, the Grizzly bear, which is the only species of bear known to attack at night time if it feels so inclined. In Asia (and formerly in Europe) they have *Ursus arctos*, the brown bear; *Ursus tibetanus*, the Himalayan black bear; and two forms related to the latter, with names that do not need explanation: *Ursus japonicus* and *Ursus malayanus*. In the far north, there is *Thalarctos maritimus*, the polar bear, which can reach a weight of 1500 pounds. The polar bear is the only bear that is exclusively a meat-eater, since fish and seal is all he can get. All the other bears are decidedly omnivorous, though meat forms a large part of their diet.

That bears are missing in the African fauna is quite surprising, just on the strength of the distribution of the bear tribe otherwise. It is even more surprising if you know one additional factor. During the last century, a veritable treasure of fossil bones was found in Greece near a shepherd's settlement called Pikermi, not far from the much better known Marathon. The Pikermi fossils are fossils of mammals. They are about seven million years old, belonging to the early part of the Pliocene sub-period of the Tertiary period. The fossils found at Pikermi indicate clearly that species of mammals which had evolved in southwestern Asia and in Europe were then migrating to Africa. There were various forms of hyenas, antelopes, elephants, and horse-like animals.

And among the Pikermi fossils—fossils—but also known from Persia and India—is an ancestor of the later bears. Its scientific name is *Hyaenarctos* and it was about the size of the smaller bears of our time. We are confronted with the strange fact that all the tribes of mammals which lived in southeastern Europe and-southwestern Asia reached Africa—except the bears. And, of course, there is no conceivable reason why the bears, who are doing very well indeed everywhere else, should not thrive in Africa.

Having explained some of the zoological background, it only remains to get rid of a linguistic confusion before we can proceed to a few of the Nandi bear stories.

The confusing fact is that the stories that have come out of central Africa ever since about 1910 deal with two different animals, both evidently mammals, both unknown and, unfortunately, with somewhat similar names. The Nandi bear is one of them. Its name was coined by the British and is taken from the name of the people who live in the area. (The Nandi themselves refer to the animal as *chemosit*.) The name of the other unknown animal is Nunda, which is a simplification of the native term *mngwa*. Mngwa is, in turn, a contraction of the Kisuaheli term *mu-ngwa*, which means "strange one." The mngwa or nunda is usually described as a lion-sized, cat-like animal with grey fur, and the stories about it all come from the coast of Tanganyika.

The descriptions of the Nandi bear, on the other hand, definitely do not suggest a feline, and the stories about it come from central Africa, mainly the Kenya region, but also from the Congo area.

Here is a typical one, told to the British anthropologist C. W. Hobley by a Major Toulson:

"It was getting dark when one of my boys came into my room and said that a leopard was close to the kitchen. I rushed out at once and saw a strange beast making off. It appeared to have long hair behind and it was rather low in front. I should say it stood about 18 to 20 inches at the shoulder; it appeared to be black, with a gait similar to that of a bear—a kind of shuffling walk. Unfortunately it was nearly dark at the time and I did not get a fair view of the head.

"Several Dutchmen had asked me a few days before what the strange animal was on the plateau; they said it was like a bear, but they had only seen it at dusk; it turned on their dogs and chased them off. They described it as a thick-set beast, and it was making a peculiar moaning cry."

The date of that story is 1912.

Some twenty years later, Captain A. T. A. Ritchie, who was the game warden of what was then the Kenya Protectorate, collected Nandi bear reports which were actually incorporated in the Annual Report for 1935 of the Game Department of the protectorate.

A typical one, told to Captain Ritchie by a Mr. Anderssen, reported that Mr. Anderssen went out on a rainy day because of excited noises made by a group of natives whom he found standing around a dead and disemboweled pig. At that moment he heard a roar from the forest and he tried to get the men to go with him to pursue the beast, but the men refused; they were not going to go any nearer the "devil" than they were at the moment. Questioned about the appearance, those who said they had seen it agreed on long black fur and a head that was not very big, but *baya sana.*

"As regards black hair," Mr. Anderssen continued, "we found long black hair lost in the battle; this was not from the pig, which had coarser hair. The boys could not explain in what way the head was *baya sana* but they all agreed that it was 'very bad.' I could not get a clear footmark in the grass. What I could see looked very large, something like the mark of an old leopard which could not draw in its claws properly. The pig appeared to have been killed in an extraordinary manner, as if it had been hit, say, with a log, breaking the backbone; it had then been turned over and the stomach torn open with powerful claws. The stomach, heart, etc. had been eaten."

The fact that the internal organs had been eaten and nothing else, unfortunately, is not indicative of a particular predatory animal. Most carnivores, after a kill, will begin their feast with the internal organs of the victim, and then go on to the larger muscles. In this particular case the predator, whatever it was, probably was scared off, which would account for the condition of the dead pig.

But there seems to be a general feeling among the natives that the feeding habits of the Nandi bear are somehow unusual and strange. Whenever a corpse of a man with a smashed skull is discovered by somebody, the Nandi bear will get the blame. It is supposed to lie flat on low branches waiting for somebody to come along. Then one blow of its clawed paw will smash the skull and the Nandi bear will eat the brain. There is even a special word for it which means "brain eater."

An actual case of such a brain-eater was described in 1919 by a farmer named Buxton:

"Its first appearance was on my farm, where the sheep were missing. We finally found all ten, seven dead and three still alive. In no case were the bodies touched, but the brains were torn out ... During the next ten days, fifty-seven goats and sheep were destroyed in the same way; of these thirteen were found alive. The Lumbwa were all in a state of great terror, and weird stories were told about the brain-eater, how it walked on its hind legs, pulled babies out of huts, and was even able to kill a man. Finally it was tracked to a ravine and killed by the Lumbwa with their spears. It turned out to be a very large hyena of the ordinary spotted variety. It had evidently turned brain-eater through some sort of madness."

The fact that the men tracked and killed a very large hyena, however, does not make the case completely clear. Hyenas have no paws which could tear the top off the skull of a sheep or goat in order to get at the brain. And if old hyenas turned brain-eaters, that fact would be known, just as it is known the old lions and tigers turn man-eater. But if the killings had been done by another animal, it is very likely that hyenas were attracted by the presence of the corpses of the victims.

The investigation of the Nandi bear stories is made more difficult by the fact that the Nandi themselves use their word *chemosit* in more than one sense. It is not just a name for an animal which they know and for which the white man has no name since he does not know it. It is a word which also means something like "demon." The word is used to scold children into submission, and inquisitive travelers are supplied with curious detail, such as that the chemosit has long whiskers and that its urine smells so bad the dogs run away from it and no man can force himself to remain near it.

It is detail like this that has prompted conservative zoologists to discredit the whole story of the Nandi bear and which has, on the other hand, caused less conservative zoologists to explain the Nandi bear by assuming the existence of a giant mandrill at least as large as a man, while still others have invented a giant hyena for the purpose. Such explanations disregard the simple fact that a land-roving animal is less likely to remain unknown the larger it is.

To find an animal, real or hypothetical, which fits all the descriptions of the Nandi bear is impossible, for the very simple reason that the descriptions to which this name has been attached are descriptions of several different animals. Some of the reports almost certainly refer to old, large, and solitary hyenas. In other cases the deeds of leopards were attributed to the unknown animal. One careful, if scared, description is indubitably that of an aardvark seen suddenly at night by a man who never had seen a live aardvark before. A good number of the alleged misdeeds of the Nandi bear look to a skeptical observer as if they were simple murderss, committed for some unknown reasons without any witnesses and later slightly disguised so that they would be blamed on an attack by a predator.

Even if all these things are discounted, there remains a set of statements which refer to a bear, which is to say, to something that looks like a bear, even though, zoologically speaking, it may not be a bear at all.

Now it so happens that there is a mammal in Africa that would make a fine Nandi bear if only it were larger.

It is comparatively rare and because of its habits—usually nocturnal and burrowing—it is very rarely seen.

The animal goes under a small collection of names. It is called African honey-eater (its scientific name is *Mellivora*, which means the same) or African honey-badger, and the customary name among English naturalists is ratel. As for the other names, one feels like paraphrasing Voltaire's famous statement that the Holy Roman Empire wasn't holy, wasn't Roman, and wasn't even an empire, by saying that the African honey-badger is not really a badger, that its main food isn't honey, but that it is, at least, African.

The ratel is one of the family of carnivores to which the badgers belong and which numbers among its members the wolverine (also called "glutton") of the Arctic, which has been called the most voracious and bloodthirsty of this generally bloodthirsty group. Every naturalist has remarked on the fact that the wolverine looks like a bear cub, and this applies to the ratel, too.

The ratel's body is, in a fully grown specimen, almost precisely one yard long, to which an eight-inch tail is to be added. It is very sturdily and powerfully built, has strong claws (not retractable) and a set of teeth which can do almost as much damage as the teeth of a wolf. Its long fur is black, except for the back, where it is silvery white.

One fact about the ratel, significant when it comes to Nandi bear stories, is that the white portions of the fur disappear with age and are replaced by black fur, except for a crescent-shaped marking above and between the eyes which remains white.

If by now you begin to wonder whether Hans Schomburgk's *Too* (after all, he did not see it himself,

218

but was just given a description) was just an old ratel, we are in complete agreement.

While the ratel does like honey, it is omnivorous and mainly carnivorous; it hunts for mice, birds, snakes, and large snails. It looks for fruit and fleshy roots, and for ground-nesting bees. It will break into chicken coops and even kill a young deer on occasion. Its thick fur and tough skin are like armor, but when it encounters a superior enemy like a leopard or a large dog the ratel tries to escape without a fight. Its strong claws enable it to dig with fantastic speed. Observers have said that a ratel, even in medium hard stony soil, appears to sink into the earth, disappearing under the surface like a diving submarine.

If the ground is too hard to do that, it still has another weapon: the same weapon as the skunk, to which it is distantly related. The Dutch naturalist van Arkel d'Ablaing said that he put two rifle bullets into a ratel one night from a distance of less than twenty paces, but the animal escaped in the dark and since it started to rain, van Arkel waited until the next morning. "Looking for it the next day in the underbrush was simple; all I had to do was to follow my nose. The rain that had fallen had diminished the stench but failed to destroy it; the stench was still so horrible that only my scientific zeal made me keep up the search."

But if even the stink glands do not enable the ratel to do what it wants to do, namely to be left alone, it will turn into a ferocious fighter. There is no report that a ratel ever killed a man, but it seems reasonably certain that an unarmed man would be wise to run away at full speed if confronted with a thoroughly aroused, full-grown ratel.

The ratel, then, has all qualifications but one for the Nandi bear stories: it is nocturnal, it is rarely seen, it looks like a bear, it is carnivorous, it is powerfully built and can be dangerous, it even can produce a nauseating stench. If the normal length of an adult ratel were five feet instead of three, nobody could entertain any doubts about the identity of Nandi bear and ratel. As it is, one has to conclude that any killings of livestock or people that are unusual in some respect are habitually attributed to the unknown and the ratel, on the rare occasions it is seen, is taken to be this unknown.

It is even possible that an occasional solitary, old ratel grows to an unusual size. In spite of the fact that the animal is not very rare, actually very little about its habits is known.

The Nandi bear problem has two possible solutions.

One is that it is not an unknown animal at all, but rather it is a case of mistaken identity in which old ratels have been blamed for things they didn't do. This mistake is possible because the habits of the ratel seem to be better known to people working in zoological gardens far from the scene than to the people who live where it lives.

The other possible solution, which grows less and less likely with passing years, is that the Nandi bear is not yet known to science. If you feel inclined to believe this, you may start wondering all over again why there are no bears in Africa.

Phantom Panther on the Prowl

Loren Coleman
November 1977

Most of the publicity surrounding the Richland Township, Ohio, killings began after Sherwood Burkholder was interviewed by Dayton TV-7 and other local media. On April 25, 1977, Burkholder had lost forty sheep to some unknown animal killer. On the 26th he lost another seventeen sheep.

William Reeder, Dog Warden and Executive Director of the Allen County Humane Society, had been investigating such killings for more than a month before Burkholder's sheep were attacked. Reeder was the person most often quoted in the press, and it was with him that I spent the better part of June 29, 1977, discussing the problem. It was Reeder who told me the Burkholder sheep had been grabbed at the rear of their jaws and then clawed forward. Eight claw marks were visible on the sheep's sides. Although most of the sheep were not dead when Reeder arrived on the scene, he had to destroy all of them. Later he went back and took plaster casts of what he believed were the killer's tracks.

The Burkholder sheep were kept in a large pen located near Tom Fett and Rockport Roads. The killer struck before dawn the first time, then early the next day, and finally the afternoon of that same day.

I talked with Carol Benson, who rents a trailer that sits on Burkholder's land—Sherwood Burkholder lives on a farm many miles north. She said she did not hear a thing. It was not until a month later that Carol Benson, her son Bryan, and Burkholder saw a large, black cat stalking back and forth among the trees near the creek out back.

By the time I visited the Burkholder land, next to Benson's trailer, no sheep were around because the owner had decided not to restock that land, and to keep his other 250 head at his northern farm, nearer his own residence.

While the Burkholder story got most of the media coverage, the killings at the Elmer Nesbaum farm earlier in March are more interesting from an investigative and human point of view.

On March 22, 1977, something got into Elmer Nesbaum's sheep. Through my interviews with William Reeder, and with Mr. and Mrs. Elmer Nesbaum, I was able to reconstruct the events as follows:

Elmer Nesbaum, 74, and his wife, who are Reformed Mennonites, lived on a ninety-four-acre farm on Napoleon Road near the Columbus Grove-Bluffton Road, a couple of miles northwest of Burkholder's land. On this particular windy and snowy March night, Elmer Nesbaum had penned his sheep because most of them were about ready to lamb. He liked sheep; they were easy to keep and these sheep had become his friends; they all would crowd around him when he came to see them.

"When I came in the first morning," Nesbaum told me, "only a few were standing. They were all red and I wondered what happened with these sheep.

Something terrible went on in there! It was a bad sight to see."

What Nesbaum found was a "bloody mess" at the end of the pen. He called a veterinarian and had what sheep could be saved sewed up. Then he prepared for another assault. His sheep were housed in a pen at the back of a U-shaped area between his barn and his machine and lofting sheds. Nesbaum put heavy farm gates across the front of the pen, regular wire fencing up to the roof of the barn, and then chicken wire on the top. He put six steel muskrat traps in front of the pen.

When the killer came back on March 26, it set off all six traps and clawed the gates apart, leaving chunks of wood marked by teeth and claws. When I inspected the area, the one-foot to two-foot pieces of wood still lay where Nesbaum had found them on the 26th; he had not moved a thing. Nesbaum gave me several wood chunks out of which many semicircular bites had been taken and on which fang-like punctures are quite visible. Nesbaum said he had found clumps of black and blackish-brown hair sticking to the fencing, but he did not keep them, thinking it was not important. "I didn't realize it was goin' to become such a mystery," Elmer told me.

As Bill Reeder described it to me, the animal had "literally clawed the Nesbaum sheep; it didn't eat the sheep, didn't hamstring the sheep, didn't gut the sheep. It just put eight perfect claw marks down the sides— from the backbone to the stomach. One of the ewes had her udder completely torn off. Also," Reeder continued, "there was fang marks across the neck. Definitely punctures, two on each side." That was after the first attack. The second time Reeder noticed "only clawing, no biting. The only one with fang marks was a lamb which had been born between the first and second attacks. It had the four perfect fang marks. The vet tried to save it, but its rib cage was crushed."

Because the pen was on a concrete slab covered by straw, Reeder and the Nesbaums found only one track. In all, the Nesbaums lost twenty sheep, most of them pregnant.

For Elmer Nesbaum and his wife, the events of late March 1977 were a personal tragedy. They had been looking forward to selling their sheep and new lambs, disposing of the farm, and retiring to a smaller place. Mrs. Nesbaum had been ill during the winter and Elmer wanted to move closer to town. The killings ended their hopes. Nesbaum felt he was "out of the business, but you hate it to go out like that."

Elmer Nesbaum spoke to me of his affection for his sheep, and Bill Reeder told me how the couple had stood there and cried. They finally went back into their farmhouse; they couldn't watch Reeder destroy their sheep.

Mrs. Nesbaum tried to be philosophical when she was talking to me. She said softly, "Well, it's a mystery. The thing'll never be solved."

After the Nesbaum and Burkholder sheep were killed, Bill Reeder found events moving more rapidly. On the first of May, five sheep were killed at the Richard Etter farm on Pandora Road. Two days later, Herman Hilty of Lugabill Road lost some tame ducks. At the Hilty farm, Reeder found and took more casts of what he was beginning to feel were cat tracks. The Hilty casts exactly match the casts taken at the Burkholder place but, although cat-like, these tracks show the now-familiar, nonretractable claw marks.

Bill Reeder got still other reports of sheep killings from Phillips Road. The killer appeared to be moving south down that road toward the town of Lafayette. At about the same time the killings increased, reports of actual sightings of a large cat began to come in. Bill Reeder pulled out a stack of reports and started reading them to me.

April 28—Maria Henderson was the first person to report seeing the cat. In her statement to Bluffton police, she said she was on her way to work on Bentley Road, near County Line Road, when she saw what she thought was a dog in the road. When she got closer, she saw it was a cat. Finally, she got out of her car and walked to within four feet of it. She reported that it definitely was a cat ... a big cat, approximately one-and-one-half-feet tall, black and gray in color. The Bluffton police know Maria Henderson to be a "good, substantial, solid citizen."

April 29—Bob Cross, an employer at the Lima State Hospital and member of the local news media, watched a large black cat for ten minutes.

May 1—The "glassy eyes of a cat" were spotted by a deputy with a spotlight at 2:30 A.M. near Lafayette. Reeder later found tracks resembling the others.

May 6—Lou Abial of Napoleon Road went out to his barn at about 6:45 P.M., and when he returned he saw cat tracks which had not been there a moment before. Reeder said it appeared the cat had jumped from the hayloft. They followed the tracks to the end of Abial's property, but never saw the animal.

May 9—At 7:30 A.M. Barbara Price reported seeing a huge black and gray cat with a big head and a long tail cross in front of her car on Highway 81 near Swaney

Road. Two off-duty deputies and Reeder searched the area for two hours and found many tracks, but failed to locate the cat. On this same day, Mr. Rutherford of 9890 Reservoir Road found tracks on his property.

May 12—An Allen County veterinarian found fang marks on the neck of a dead German shepherd.

By mid-May the sheep killer was getting big play in the local newspapers. Whatever it was, it was being held responsible for killing five peacocks, some tame ducks, a German shepherd, and at least 140 head of sheep, and William Reeder found he had hold of a hot political potato. Allen County Sheriff Charles Harrod called Reeder into his office and more or less told him they were taking over the investigations. The sheriff believed the killings were being done by a pack of dogs, and Reeder's findings were making him uncomfortable.

About the same time, Reeder was confronted by the sheriff's dog-pack theories, the cat "woke up half of Lafayette" at 1:15 A.M. one morning.

On May 17, two residents in the Lafayette area reported seeing a large, dark-colored cat drinking from their pond.

Despite the sheriff's theories, Reeder was more and more convinced a large black and gray feline was the culprit. On May 20, he held a news conference at which he announced his conclusions and detailed the mounting body of evidence. Besides the sightings and footprints, Reeder also had found some droppings on the farm next to the Burkholder place which he had given to Dr. Wayne Kaufman and Dr. R. L. McMahn, veterinarians practicing in Lima, Ohio. The silver-dollarsized feces were found to contain balls of hair and hookworms, all characteristic of cat scat. After examining the droppings and hearing of the manner of the sheep kills, Dr. McMahn said to Reeder, "Bill, this is a panther-type animal."

After this William Reeder was told not to hold any more news conferences.

On May 27, the mayor of Lafayette called Reeder and told him the cat was in Lafayette. Reeder and another officer joined the mayor and two Lafayette police officers, but failed to locate the animal.

As soon as Bill got home he received another call. This time it was the manager of a lakeside resort and camping area southeast of Lafayette. He said the cat was drinking from a swimming hole near the campgrounds, but asked Reeder not to go down there because it might panic the campers. Reeder said he determined that the cat was not bothering anyone so he did not go after it.

The Allen County dog warden sat down to a cup of coffee and tried to relax after what seemed like another in a series of hectic days, but his phone rang. It was the Lafayette police again, and they had the cat in sight in a plowed field near Lafayette. Bill Reeder raced out there. It was 2:00 A.M. by then, and Reeder, an off-duty sheriff's deputy, and two Lafayette police officers were using large flashlights and spotlights. The deputy circled around into the nearby woods. They all had a pretty good view of the animal and slowly began walking toward the cat. When they were within thirty-five yards of it, the cat calmly began to walk toward them "like it was going to be a docile animal," Reeder said. But when it was only about twenty yards away, "within tranquilizer gun range," all of a sudden it broke for the woods. It ran "150 yards in two minutes flat," Reeder told me.

As it went into the woods, it was sighted by the deputy stationed there—then it was gone.

Bill Reeder's description matches the descriptions supplied by the other witnesses in the area. He said it was black, one and one-half to two feet tall, and had "the pointed ears of a cat." He could not see the animal's tail, but he felt its "movement was that of a cat not of a dog." In the lights, the animal's glassy eyes appeared to be gold or yellow.

After the cat escaped into the woods, Reeder found tracks with claw marks exactly like those in the Hilty-Burkholder casts.

William Reeder was forbidden to give a news release on this sighting and no local publications have run stories on it. I am the first writer with whom he discussed the incidents of May 27. Reeder is a no-nonsense sort of fellow who has taken a good deal of flak because of his "big black cat" theory.

The sheep killer seems to have left Allen County, Ohio. During the first week of June, the newspapers carried articles on the sighting of a "large black cat" near the town of Ada, ten miles due east of Lafayette, in Hardin County.

Hancock County Game Protector Brad Lindsey and Hardin County Game Protector Gary Braun went out looking for the cat because of reports from Ada area residents. Braun was quoted as saying he got a good look at the animal and it was definitely large and black and feline. Braun watched the cat for twelve to twenty seconds through field glasses before it walked off into the woods. No livestock have been killed in Hardin County.

So what are we to do?

Here again we find a large cat in an area where pumas (which are not supposed to be black) have been extinct for over 100 years. Students of Forteana will recognize the almost classic nature of this 1977 Ohio mystery cat—its elusiveness, its clawed footprints, its savage attacks on livestock, and the overwhelming number of firsthand sightings. Allen County, Ohio, seems to have entertained our old friend, the phantom panther, a creature which has no business existing, but seems to do so anyway.

1977 proved to be a synchronistically interesting year for the mystery cats. One hundred years earlier, 1877 saw numerous mystery cat reports from Ohio and Indiana. So far this year, besides the Ohio sightings, there have been sightings in Bay Springs, Mississippi, Edwardsville, Illinois, and in California and Kentucky.

Author's Note: I wish to thank Mark A. Hall, Tom Adams and David Fideler for background articles which I found helpful, and my thanks go to William Reeder, Mr. and Mrs. Elmer Nesbaum, and Carol Benson for the interviews they granted me.

Tracking Tasmania's Mystery Beast

Michael Goss
July 1983

The story of the thylacine (popularly known as the Tasmanian wolf or Tasmanian tiger) reached its sad end on Monday, September 7, 1936, when "Benjamin," the last captive specimen, died in the Hobart Domain Zoo. Ironically, the death occurred less than two months after the passage of a Tasmanian law protecting his species.

To all appearances the thylacine had gone the way of the dodoes and the dinosaurs. Always mysterious, it soon became almost a myth. Yet, as we know, myths sometimes come to life.

One afternoon in 1971, a man stalking deer in the high country of eastern Tasmania practically stepped on a doglike creature whose sandy-colored coat bore one and one-half-inch wide dark stripes across its back and two-thirds of the way down its sides. The strange animal's head actually brushed the hunter's gun barrel as it raced away, the deer scattering wildly before it. Had he not known that thylacine were extinct, the hunter would have thought he had just seen one. He was left to conclude that he had encountered either a deformed dog or some bizarre cross between a Tasmanian devil and one of the island's feral canines.

When he later saw a stuffed thylacine in a museum, however, the man changed his mind. Now he was certain he had crossed paths with a thylacine.

The year before, in fact, no fewer than six persons had watched an animal the size of a sheep dog, with thick striped fur, cross a road between Launceston and Scottsdale a little after midnight. They too believed they had seen a thylacine.

In 1980, in an incident reminiscent of the deer hunter's experience, a senior timber worker disturbed a creature apparently resting on a steep hillside, in an area in which no dogs were reported either before or after the incident. Its lightish-gray hair carried between three and five dark bars from the midback to the base of its stiff straight tail.

Is it possible that thylacines still live?

With a maximum length of up to six feet from the muzzle of its foxlike head to the tip of its curiously stiff inflexible tail, the thylacine was indeed the marsupial equivalent of the wolf. (Its scientific name, *Thylacinus cynocephalus*, means "the pouched dog with a wolf's head.") Despite its wolflike appearance, the animal to which the thylacine was most closely related was the opossum; the two apparently shared a common ancestor.

The thylacine was not a member of the huge and varied dog family at all. When it gaped its jaws at an incredible 120 (some say as much as 150) degree angle, the zoologist might notice eight upper incisors—two more than the six found in canines. Besides less obvious anatomical differences, no dog possesses the powerfully developed hindquarters which enabled the thylacine to assume an upright, kangaroolike posture for short periods. Perhaps this was nature's way of compensating for the animal's inability to wag its tail like a dog.

But if thylacines were not wolves, nonetheless they filled the same ecological niche—that of large dog predators—as wolves. The thylacines evolved in such a way that their habits and even physical characteristics mimicked those of independent nonrelated species (wolf, coyote, dingo, or jackal) occurring in other parts of the world.

The popular name by which the thylacine is known, "Tasmanian tiger," is misleading. Thylacines are not tiger-cats (which are not true cats) or Tasmanian devils—stocky, ferocious-looking animals about the size of a small dog. Both of these are marsupial carnivores, but neither much resembles the larger, more striking and allegedly extinct thylacines. Finally, the thylacine must not be confused with the other cryptozoological enigma, the "Queensland tiger," a phantom feline from the Australian mainland that has itself been the subject of considerable controversy.

Except for zoologists, Tasmanians were slow to accept the idea that a species as hardy as the thylacines had vanished from the face of the earth. After all, the animal had made survival its specialty from the Quaternary period onwards. Ousted from the mainland (it is generally thought) by the dingo—a more efficient predator, faster breeder, and less choosy eater—the thylacine found a final refuge in the small island at the southeastern heel of Australia. It was well-distributed throughout all but southwestern Tasmania, preferring dry, densely vegetated hill regions or moist sclerophyll-rain forest districts where it thrived on the smaller marsupials. Later its menu expanded to include sheep. That proved to be a fatal mistake.

Sheep arrived with the first white settlers in 1803. Within thirty-five years the Tasmanian sheep population topped one million.

The landowners who claimed that thylacines were decimating their sheep herds may have been exaggerating; harsh weather and overstocking were also taking their toll. Nonetheless, such complaints led, in 1830, to the Van Diemen's Land Company's offering a bounty for dead thylacines. In the 1880s, farmers petitioned Parliament to institute a government-sanctioned bounty. Spokesman John Lyne told Parliament that up to 70,000 sheep had been lost, mostly to thylacines, and that he personally could not put a single sheep on his 2,000 acres. In reality, predators such as dogs and "duffers" (rustlers, who were stealing up to 100 sheep a night) were a far greater problem to farmers than thylacines.

Between 1879 and 1909, according to an official tally, nearly 5,000 thylacines were shot, trapped, or otherwise destroyed and claimed for private and government bounty, but that does not represent the total number killed; considerably more of the animals were claimed for local bounties and so did not appear in the official figures.

Even so, in some areas the thylacine population did not decline. Although from 1892 to 1902 bounty payments were made for more than 100 adults, somehow the thylacines resisted the thrust toward extinction, but that abruptly changed during the first decade of the twentieth century. From 153 bounty claims in 1900, the numbers dropped in only nine years to a mere two. The thylacines were apparently no longer there to be harvested at the rate of one pound an adult, 10 shillings a juvenile.

What happened, apparently, was this: the thylacine (in common with other carnivorous marsupials) suffered the ravages of a viral disease like distemper. If this alone had been its problem, it could have survived, but the long years of hunting to which the thylacine had been subjected had depleted the resiliency of the breed. Always vulnerable to competition, its habitat greatly reduced and under pressure from all directions, the breeding capability of the species was wiped out and the thylacine was brought to extinction.

As late as 1928, some sheep owners still protested moves to place the thylacine on the list of protected Tasmanian species. People simply could not believe the animal was in danger. Soon they were speculating that surely it must be surviving in remote unpopulated areas.

Since 1936, naturalists have reluctantly thought otherwise. They take no delight in this conclusion, however, and would be only too happy to be proven wrong. Every decade at least one expedition, composed either of zoologists or lay enthusiasts, sets off into obscure corners of the Tasmanian bush, hoping to find a living thylacine. So far, none of these endeavors has met with success.

But if hard evidence has been lacking, tantalizing anecdotal accounts suggest that something may be out there. Those who have gone looking for it haven't found it, but—if their reports are to be believed—unsuspecting persons have accidentally confronted the very thing the experts can't find.

Steven Smith of Tasmania's National Parks and Wildlife Service has collected 320 reports of possible thylacine sightings for the "post-extinction" years 1936–1980. By his standards, only 107 are "good" reports. While he believes the sighting peaks are related to publicity surrounding expeditions to find the animal, nonetheless he observes that "the number of reported sightings per decade has risen markedly since 1936." Seventy percent of them date from the years 1960-1980 alone, with "crests" for 1970 (29 sightings), 1971 (19), and 1980 (19 cases up until November).

According to Smith, the witnesses form a broad spectrum of the types of people one might expect to penetrate the backcountry regions where the thylacine may yet survive. Persons living or working in the sighting area constitute the highest number (187), with shooters, bush walkers, tourists, anglers, and others making up the 258 total.

A "typical" thylacine sighting features a solitary witness meeting a solitary animal, but there are reports of two, three and even five thylacines; likewise there are reports made by multiple human witnesses, one of them involving eight persons.

Smith's findings suggest that you would be most likely to see a thylacine in the northern half of the state and in country up to 650 feet above sea level. Occasional sightings have been made along beaches. On Tasmania's west coast, for example, Gary Clarke saw what he believed was a thylacine on January 29, 1973; even at sixty-five feet, the witness could plainly see the black stripes on the sandy hide, as well as the stiffly-held tail. By the time Clarke managed to fetch his camera, the unexpected visitor was gone.

Most sightings (sixty-five percent) have occurred at night (between 6:00 P.M. and 6:00 A.M.). In one of the more unusual of these, on July 15, 1980, twenty-two-year-old Gavin How and two companions were out in the forest near Mole Creek, where How worked at a wildlife park. In the darkness the headlights on their van picked out a pair of eyes some 100 yards ahead; a spotlight revealed an orange-gold animal with black stripes and head like a German shepherd dog's. Apparently unconcerned, the animal scratched its belly with a forepaw—not something one would expect a dog to do—and allowed the three witnesses to come within ten yards. They were so close, they later claimed, that they could easily have captured the animal. They didn't do so, needless to say.

David Yendall, who describes this incident in the May 1982 issue of *Britain's Wildlife,* says he heard of other thylacine sightings around Mole Creek. Witnesses kept quiet, not because they feared ridicule, but because they were concerned that hunting rights in the area would be rescinded if the authorities learned of the presence of a rare animal.

From Steven Smith's analysis we are more likely to conclude that motorists, who comprise fifty-five percent of the witnesses, pose a greater threat to thylacines than hunters do, but so far as we know no thylacine has been struck and killed by a car.

If the people who think they have seen thylacines are mistaken, just what have they seen? Since the reports stress the animals' canine appearance, that rules out wallabies, wombats, and other exotic Australian fauna. Foxes and dingoes aren't found in Tasmania. The Tasmanian devil has no stripes and the banded anteater, although striped, is too small, lives in western Australia, and does not go out at night.

The only reasonable alternative explanation then, is that the "tigers" are feral dogs, perhaps crossbreeds. Wild dogs once were common on the island; according to Van Diemen's Land Company records between 1832 and 1849 wild dogs killed twice as many sheep (299) in the Surrey Hills as did thylacines (147), but today wild dogs are too rare to account for all the known sightings of supposed thylacines. Since these incidents occur away from settlements, the possibility that domestic canines are masquerading as tigers seems remote.

Of course it would be naive to contend that witnesses never make mistakes, but the scientists who have investigated the reports have made their share of mistakes as well.

In 1957, a sensational—but ultimately disappointing—episode occurred. In October of that year, Eric Guiler, then Reader in Zoology at the University of Tasmania, accompanied G. K. Meldrum, from the Department of Agriculture, to the pastoral country of the Derwent Valley not far from Hobart, where a predator had slain several sheep. The killer had wrenched their throats and lower faces, but left the rest of the carcass untouched.

This seemed to eliminate the Tasmanian devil. Even if the animal were a sheep killer (which it isn't), it would scarcely have passed so tempting a store of meat. A dog, the investigators felt, would not have stopped short at a single night's depredations and only a handful of victims. Dr. Guiler knew of the thylacine's reputation as a most fastidious feeder which did not return to a kill, and he thought the *modus operandi* appeared suspiciously akin to that creature's style of hunting.

Then there were mysterious tracks which did not correspond to those of the devil, native cat, wombat, or dog—but they did resemble impressions taken from thylacine specimens in a local museum. Moreover, the owner of an adjoining property claimed to have seen a thylacine at least twice. "The evidence here," Guiler wrote in the *Australian Journal of Science* for March-April 1958, "led us to conclude that a thylacine or thylacines were not only in the area, but probably were responsible for the sheep killings."

The unglamorous sequel to the Dervent Valley story came when a large dog was caught in a trap. With it, the sheep killings ceased. The experts dropped the idea that the thylacine had made a gory comeback. They were unimpressed by an indistinct photograph taken from a helicopter flying over the west coast during a mining survey in January 1957; they concluded that the animal in the picture was probably just a large dog.

Zoologists typically demand a carcass, preferably a fresh one, before they will concede the existence of a continuous animal. On the night of August 1961, it looked as if they were about to get one when two fishermen clubbed to death a creature raiding their bait hut at Sandy Cape (again on the west coast). Although the body mysteriously vanished, Guiler declared that hair tufts scraped from the floor were from a young male thylacine. Almost twenty years later, however, a taped interview with one of the witnesses quelled all hope that the Sandy Cape episode proved the thylacine's reappearance. The witness said that at the time he had been unfamiliar with Tasmanian wildlife, but now he is absolutely positive that he and his friend killed a Tasmanian devil, not a Tasmanian tiger.

Most scientists concerned with the thylacine controversy rest their hopes on the well-organized expeditions that periodically search for the elusive beast, but repeated ventures into the bush have done little to improve on the first expedition's discovery of tracks in the northwest in May 1937. Many probers, for instance Sarland and Fleming (1938), and David Fleay (1945-46), returned home convinced by tracks and sighting reports that the thylacine survived, but such conviction counted little next to the demand for hard data to support that conclusion.

In the wake of the 1961 Sandy Cape affair, farmer Reuben Charles sent Guiler a hair sample from what he thought might be a thylacine lair on his Mawbanna property. From external scale patterns of this sample, Guiler deduced that the hair did indeed come from a thylacine, but Hans Brunner of the Keith Turnbull Research Station in Victoria examined other samples taken at the same time and concluded otherwise. Traps were set at the site over the next two months, but the animal refused to cooperate. It was never captured, so the dispute between the two authorities was never resolved.

Malley and Griffith tried a different tactic. They experimented with automatic camera monitoring over the course of several expeditions between 1968 and 1972. Even with twenty-five cameras spread across Northern Tasmania, the object of their efforts remained coyly invisible. The scientists studied tracks and listened to witnesses' testimony, but got no closer to the thing responsible for them.

Throughout 1980 and 1981, the Tasmanian National Parks and Wildlife Service tried to settle the issue once and for all. Supported by $55,000 from the World Wildlife Fund-Australia, it arranged a two-pronged expedition. Steven Smith and trainee ranger Adrian Pyrke set up three still-camera units at seventeen sites selected after computer analysis of over 200 thylacine reports throughout the whole country; the idea was for a range of baits (meat-meal, raw wallaby, and cooked ham were the most effective) to lure animals into breaking an infrared light beam across selected game trails, triggering a 35mm camera with motor-drive attachment and bulk film magazine, plus flashgun. As a general exercise in wildlife photography, it proved spectacularly successful—422 species were captured, 364 of them showing our old friend the Tasmanian devil, but not one thylacine posed for the camera.

Smith defends the project as "an initial survey of some of the more promising locations," and he says that longer surveillance periods might produce better results. The knowledge that it provided of native fauna was valuable in itself; yet the critics who had suggested that the WWF-Australia might find better ways to spend $55,000 were not mollified. Although no official report of the second phase of the expedition (which Dr. Guiler directed) has been released, it appears that his automatic movie-camera "stakeouts" have not been any more successful than Smith and Pyrke's. In short, surviving thylacines, if they exist, remain unphotographed and unproven.

For an animal that refused to breed in captivity, the thylacine has proved adept at breeding confusion and controversy about itself. Nothing is more calculated to raise the blood pressure of Australian zoologists than the suggestion that the marsupial wolf exists not only in Tasmania but also on the mainland, where it has previously been known only from aboriginal rock paintings, fragmentary bones, and, most remarkable of all, a mummified corpse complete with hair found in a cave near Eucla. A preserved thylacine that died over 4,500 years ago (according to radiocarbon dating) is one thing; a living, breathing one is quite another.

Disregarding misidentification (one "thylacine" run over by a car turned out to be a brindled kangaroo dog), and the irritating confusion between the pouched wolf and a host of phantom feline accounts that end in the shooting of some abnormally large multicolored dog-dingo crossbreed, many of these "impossible" mainland sightings appear neither more nor less credible than their Tasmanian counterparts.

Unlike the "Yengarie lion" (a 170-pound presumed dingo-collie cross), the "Maffra leopard" (a white-streaked, eight-foot-long dingo) or the "Tantanoola tiger" (a hopelessly out-of-place Assyrian wolf), the striped rigid-tailed animal sighted several times around Ozenkadnook, Victoria, in late 1962 has never been identified. Lang, Lang, Victoria, hosted two thylacine sightings on successive nights in November 1979, and another in January 1981. Late in 1979 a Benambra witness was "as sure as apples" that he had seen a Tasmanian tiger.

Naturalists say it is extremely unlikely that so prominent a predator as the thylacine could have gone undetected in mainland Australia, where there is no irrefutable record of its occurring within white man's living memory. Still, puzzling silence surrounds two photos published in the *Australian Sunday Telegraph* for August 8, 1976, and March 27, 1977; these purport to show individuals from a pack of eight "tigers" then under tight surveillance on the New South Wales-Victoria border. Large-pack behavior, however, isn't a noted thylacine characteristic. Furthermore, the animal in one picture seems to be flourishing its tail with a freedom unknown to the "Tassie wolf." So far as I know, no one has yet exposed these pictures as hoaxes. The optimistic may choose to borrow an argument sometimes spoken of in Tasmanian wildlife circles; that thylacines do survive in isolated communities, but the authorities (park rangers, for instance) deny it in order to protect the species.

The thylacine most recently surfaced as an issue in January 1983, when mass protests were held, intended to stop a hydroelectric dam scheme that threatened the Gordon and Franklin River area of southwestern Tasmania. Thylacines frequented the upper reaches of the Franklin in the 1920s, and in 1937 Fleming believed he had discovered tracks at eleven area sites. Among other arguments employed against the dam project, conservationists insisted it was wrong to destroy the habitat of what may be the world's rarest large mammal.

Like other parts of the world, Tasmania contains rugged, little-traveled regions in which conceivably anything could live undetected by human beings. Only thirty years ago the takahe, a large flightless bird presumed extinct for decades, was rediscovered safe and well on the southern island of New Zealand. Closer still to "tiger country," and to us in time, is the rediscovery of Leadbetter's possum; zoologists had spent half a century looking for it before the creature turned up not far from the city of Melbourne in 1961. Even large animals can vanish into obscurity, only to pop up dramatically many years after we have written them off as lost forever. Consider the kouprey, a type of primitive cattle last officially sighted in 1949, and then seen and photographed in eastern Thailand in July 1982.

So perhaps the thylacine has learned to live under cover, and beyond the reach of all but the chance intruder on its territory. Although hard evidence is lacking, and the expeditions have mostly failed, the volume of sightings over the past forty-six years forces us to at least keep an open mind on the question.

In Australia, the thylacine has achieved the status of the Loch Ness monster, and the many writers who speak of tiger sightings as analogous to UFO reports aren't indulging in mere journalistic flourishes. The transient nature of the experiences, the questions the accounts raise about witness credibility, misidentification, and so on, all have parallels in ufology—and, for that matter, in many categories of apparitional encounters. So, too, do the defensively conservative reactions of some zoologists who insist (not unreasonably) on something stronger than anecdotal evidence.

Keeping a lonely tiger vigil in a tree near the Arthur River in 1973, American naturalist Jim Sayles says that he briefly sighted a dog-sized animal that he thinks may have been a thylacine. But, he confessed in an article in *Animal Kingdom* seven years afterward, "Because of the excitement and dreamlike quality of the experience I will never be certain." That is an apt summary of how the creature continues to elude us.

Killer Kangaroo

Michael T. Shoemaker
September 1985

Phantom kangaroos hopped into the public eye in the 1970s, when a flood of sightings hit the Midwest. Much less well-known, however, is the strange affair of Tennessee's "killer kangaroo," four decades earlier.

On January 16, 1934, the *Chattanooga Daily Times* carried a front-page story headlined "Vicious Kangaroolike Animal Terrorizes Marion Settlement." The paper reported that the animal first had appeared three nights before in the community of Hamburg, near South Pittsburg, Tennessee. There it "partially devoured several German police dogs." It reappeared on the 14th, killing some dogs as well as some geese and ducks. Two witnesses described the beast. The Rev. W. J. Hancock said, "It was as fast as lightning and looked like a giant kangaroo running and leaping across the field." Frank Cobb thought it was unlike anything he had ever seen, but resembled a kangaroo.

In a subsequent report, Henry Ashmore claimed that the kangaroo had visited his yard on January 12, leaving five-clawed tracks about the size of a large man's hand. Will Patten, another witness, said he had chased the animal away, but the next day discovered the half-eaten carcass of his dog lying in the yard.

But Chief of Police A. B. Russell declared that it was all "superstition started by a mad dog." This appears to have satisfied the Associated Press, which thereafter ceased reporting the events. The farmers, however, continued to carry guns and to search the mountain. One party of twenty men tracked the animal up the mountainside, but they lost its trail near a cave.

The kangaroo also ignored Chief Russell. On the night of the 16th, it killed some geese belonging to McNeal Cooley and wounded a dog in South Pittsburg. B. Y. Conatser, a former state representative, fired several times at the animal when it attacked his dogs. Perhaps because he feared ridicule, Conatser said it looked like a "large wolf or panther," but he did remark on the unusual speed and ease with which the mystery animal jumped fences and crossed fields.

Any fear of ridicule was justified. Derisive editorials appeared in the *Philadelphia Public Ledger* and *Chicago Tribune*, prompting the *Chattanooga Daily Times* to respond vigorously, "There is absolutely no doubt about these facts ... A kangaroo-like beast visited the community and killed dogs right and left, and that's all there is to it."

The mystery was finally "solved" on January 29, thirteen days after the kangaroo's last appearance. Proclaiming "Marion 'Kangaroo' Killed by Hunters," the *Chattanooga Daily Times* published a photo of four hunters, their beagles, and an "extra large bobcat or lynx" shot the night before on Signal Mountain. In fact the photo shows a fairly ordinary bobcat, common in those mountains. Although the claimed length of fifty inches is above average, the pictured bobcat is only about knee-high (nineteen to twenty inches), which is a shorter height than normal. The given weight of forty pounds is very heavy, but it had eaten several animals that night.

The witness denied it was the kangaroo. Frank Cobb said it wasn't "large enough or brown enough." Others claimed the animal they saw "would weigh at least 150 pounds and was much larger than the wildcat killed yesterday."

There are even better reasons for rejecting this solution. Bobcats avoid dogs, and only four toes appear in their tracks. More important, Signal Mountain is about twenty miles from South Pittsburg. Between them lie two mountain ranges and two rivers.

This conventional nonexplanation shows that the story was certainly not a newspaper hoax, as some writers have suggested. A more plausible explanation is that the animal was an eastern mountain lion (whose return to the Appalachians is now generally accepted). On the other hand, lions as a rule do not feed on dogs and ducks; moreover, no claws should appear in their tracks. We must also wonder why witnesses would choose so patently absurd an animal as a kangaroo for their identification.

It may be best to remember the tantalizing, cryptic conclusion of the *Chattanooga Daily Times'* editorial, which said, "Strange creatures are likely to emerge at any time from the mountains of Tennessee and neither the vision nor veracity of those who report having beheld these creatures should be called into question."

Phantom Protectors

If some supernatural animals mean no good, others exist to protect certain persons from harm: guardian angels in canine or other animal form. Over the years *FATE* has published many of these stories. Why do these phantom protectors aid only some people, and not others? Those who have had the benefit of their protection in threatening situations usually have no idea why they have been picked out, or what or whom the ghostly canine is supposed to represent. Typically the apparition is of an unfamiliar dog—in other words, these entities do not seem to be the ghosts of beloved pets. So what are they?

Gerigio, the Phantom Dog of Turin

Robert Campion Ennen
November 1949

On a still autumn evening in the year 1852, Don Bosco, a young priest of Turin in Italy, made his way wearily home through the squalid, dangerous wastes of the Valdocco quarter. He was alone. Following behind him came slinking a burly figure armed with a large club. At a darkened section of the narrow street the slugger closed in on the priest and raised his club.

Almost simultaneously, as Don Bosco tried to ward off the heavy blow, a big, grey, wolf-like animal streaked out of the twilight and leaped at the throat of the assailant. With a savage growl it threw the man to the ground. Panic-stricken, crying for help, the marauder picked himself up and stumbled off into the rubble.

"Gerigio, Gerigio!" called Don Bosco commandingly, as the dog raced after the fleeing man. Still growling ominously, the dog halted, hesitating until the terrified man was out of sight among the ruins. Then turning and trotting back to the feet of Don Bosco, it thrust its nose into the caressing hands of the young man.

Until Don Bosco reached the Pinardi house where he lived, the dog did not leave him. Then, as the door closed, it trotted off into the darkness and disappeared.

This type of incident was repeated many times for Don Bosco; a huge, grey, unknown dog appeared out of nowhere to save his life or help him through some crisis.

The first of these incidents occurred early in the autumn of 1852, and the last in 1883, covering in all a period of some thirty years, more than twice the normal span of a dog's life. The dog was called "Gerigio" because of his grey color, and was seen as far as 100 miles from Turin; he was never seen under any other circumstance than that of protector to Don Bosco. He never ate nor drank; no one ever discovered where he came from or where he went.

As a young man, Don Bosco dedicated himself to a sort of one-man youth movement—the work of making good men out of hoodlum children of Turin. By so doing he stirred up the wrath of certain persons in the city who were ready to go as far as murder to put a stop to his activities.

It was under such circumstances that the dog first entered Don Bosco's life. Gerigio's first appearance, except for the fact of his huge size, was not remarkable. There were many stray dogs roaming the city of Turin then as there are today, and when Don Bosco noticed the giant wolf-like mastiff following him, he thought nothing of it, beyond the usual apprehension one might feel in the presence of any large, stray, and undoubtedly hungry dog.

However, as the dog continued to trail along behind him, Don Bosco stopped and called to the animal. Seeming friendly enough, the dog trotted to his side and let itself be petted. When Don Bosco continued on his way again, the dog followed. It could have been nothing more than that the animal was hungry, but when Don Bosco arrived at the door of his house, Gerigio trotted off down the street without hesitation. Seeing him go, Don Bosco was a little puzzled, but thought no more about the matter as he became engrossed in his work at the hostel.

The Valdocco quarter, where the hostel was located, was the worst slum district of Turin. It was a desert of rubbish heaps and the rude shacks of drifters, crisscrossed here and there with remnants of old fences and sewers. At one end a market place attracted the dregs of the city. A few dingy taverns were gathering places for the town ruffians.

On another occasion, Don Bosco was returning home in the darkness through this quarter. As he walked down the path, two shots rang out from behind a tree near the path. Following the shots, a bandit charged out of cover and grappled with Don Bosco. Then the grey dog appeared, growling fiercely, its mane stiffened, its fangs savagely bared. It lunged at the bandit, tearing at his throat until he fled.

After that Gerigio began to appear regularly whenever Don Bosco was returning alone to the hostel. Frequently he would be found waiting outside the door as Don Bosco was about to set out on an evening errand.

One evening, as Don Bosco emerged from the hostel on a journey, he found the dog stretched across the threshold, blocking his way. Thinking Gerigio had come to accompany him, he gave the dog a friendly pat and tried to shift it out of the way. Gerigio growled ominously. Don Bosco had come to trust the dog and was dismayed to see it turn against him. Finally, seeing that it would not let him pass, he gave up the idea of the trip. Gerigio then trotted silently off into the night, leaving the priest puzzled and wondering. Moments later, a breathless friend ran up to the hostel, warning Don Bosco of an attempt on his life that was planned for that very night.

There was much conjecture about the mystery of Gerigio. It was thought that perhaps he was an angel guardian of Don Bosco, taking the form most likely to benefit him. Finally, a period of peace came into the life of Don Bosco, after a long series of these incidents, and the appearances of Gerigio ceased. To all appearances he was gone for good, but actually he was to appear twice more.

The first of these occasions occurred some ten years later, in about 1862. Don Bosco was traveling the road near the village of Castelnuovo, which is about fifty miles due east of Turin. He was on his way to the farm of friends which was located some distance outside the city, and he had been warned that the road was unsafe.

"Oh, for Gerigio!" he cried. Scarcely had he spoken when the great grey dog came bounding out of the shadows, frisking joyfully about his old friend. After ten years Gerigio had returned. Don Bosco was overjoyed. This was not the only phenomenon of the evening. When they reached the farmhouse, Gerigio was taken inside for fear of a fight with the farm dogs. There he was left in a corner while the family ate supper. Thinking of him later when the meal was over, Don Bosco collected some scraps of food, but Gerigio was gone. No door had been opened since they had come in; the windows were tight and yet Gerigio was nowhere to be found. They searched in vain through the house but he had disappeared.

Then finally, in 1883, almost thirty years after his first appearance, when he was all but forgotten, Gerigio appeared once again, this time far to the south of Turin near the coastal town of Bordighera. Don Bosco was traveling again. He was lost, when out of the night came Gerigio to assist him. After this he was never seen again. Providence had apparently decreed his work was done.

My Guardian Dog that Disappeared

Mai Packwood
November 1956

T he strangest thing I've ever experienced happened to me in February, 1928, when my second child, Verne, was three weeks old. My first girl was nearing her third birthday. My husband, Tom, worked nights, usually getting home around 2:15 A.M. My mornings were spent keeping the babies quiet so he could get his rest, and for the most part my household tasks had to be done at night.

It was not unusual for me to be either hanging out or bringing in the wash near midnight. This February night I was bringing in the wash at a little past 11:00 P.M. I heard the lock on the kitchen door snap shut behind me with a very loud click. I was conscious of the click because I was not in the habit of locking the door. I went in and out regularly and I was not afraid, despite the many warnings of my neighbors about locking my doors at night. Now the click of the back door seemed an ominous reminder to me that I had not locked the front door either.

The stillness that engulfed the house was something I had never felt before. Somehow the very air seemed to be saying that something was about to happen. I set my laundry basket down in the bedroom where my two babies slept peacefully. I noticed the baby acted a little restless. Three-year-old Nita suddenly opened her eyes and looked around as if in fright. Seeing me standing so near, she was reassured and went back to sleep.

At that very instant I heard the heavy growl of an angry dog. The growling grew louder and I could hear a vicious gnashing of the teeth now too. It had to be a big dog! This shocked me, as we owned no dog. There were only a few dogs in our neighborhood, all of them rather small house pets.

I looked through a crack in the front door blind and from my darkened room could see, to my consternation, the biggest dog I could ever imagine. His muscles were tense; he was crouched ready to spring. In the light from the street lamp, I could see his hackles standing high on his shoulders and neck. Then I saw that he was growling his warning to an approaching intruder. A man was inching his way up my front steps.

I could not see the man's face, but everything about him spelled danger and destruction. For the first time in my life I felt fear, a deep, terrifying fear. At that moment the man put his foot on the top step and suddenly the dog was upon him. For a brief instant there was wild fury, as the man and beast rolled together down the stairs. Then the man let out a scream, wrenched himself free, and ran in panic down the street. The dog calmly walked back up onto the porch and lay down with his back to the door. His muzzle rested on his front paws as he watched the man vanish.

I was able to move once more and I turned the key in the front door lock. I wanted to go out and pet the dog, but fear would not let me.

When Tom came home at the usual hour, he asked me where I got the dog. He had seen it when he turned into the driveway. I told him of my terrifying experience as I put the steak I had just cooked on his supper plate.

Before he would take a bite, Tom had to go out and see the dog. We both stroked his head and he accepted the petting. My husband remarked that he never had seen such a huge dog. He thought we ought to try to keep him and we both hoped he would stay. Tom went back into the house and brought out his supper steak and set it before the dog who made no effort to touch it, only looking up at us with friendly eyes.

The next morning Tom got up early, but the dog was gone, and so was the steak.

Hoping to find the dog in the neighborhood, we spent most of the morning driving around looking for him anxiously. We inquired as we looked, but no one had seen such a dog. Everyone raised their eyebrows skeptically when we described his size.

We never saw the dog again. I felt that something great had passed my way unexpectedly.

When the evening paper came, I knew from what the dog had saved us. On the front page was the account of the recapture of an escaped, criminally insane man. The authorities had been searching for him for several days and had picked him up near midnight, less than a mile from our home. He had deep lacerations about his neck and shoulders which he claimed he got from a dog as big as a yearling. The authorities discredited his story about the dog's size, but would give him rabies shots nevertheless, the story said.

Extra-Terrestrials Among Us
George C. Andrews

According to a law already on the books, which may be activated whenever the government wishes to enforce it, anyone found guilty of E.T. contact is to be quarantined indefinitely under armed guard. Does that sound like the government doesn't take Extra-Terrestrials seriously? This book blows the lid off the government's cover-up about UFOs and their occupants, setting the stage for a "Cosmic Watergate."

Author George Andrews researched the evidence concerning E.T. intervention in human affairs for more than a decade before presenting his startling conclusions. *Extra-Terrestrials Among Us* is an exciting challenge to "orthodox" thinking and will certainly broaden your perception of the world we live in.

This well-written book presents fascinating and documented case histories of cattle mutilations, lights in the sky, circular flying machines, strange disappearances, objects falling from the sky and spontaneous combustion. You are given direct information as to why E.T.s are here, case history descriptions of the varying appearances, and what they are trying to accomplish. You will also learn how to determine whether an alien contact is beneficial or harmful.

Here also is the story of CIA involvement, Nazi contacts, Martian landings, and much more. If you believe in E.T.s, or if you're not really sure, *Extra-Terrestrials Among Us* will open your eyes to new worlds—some existing right here on earth!

0-87542-001-X

304 pp., mass market, photos, illustrations $4.95

ESP, Witches & UFOs:
The Best of Hans Holzer, Book II
Edited by
Raymond Buckland

In this exciting anthology, best-selling author and psychic investigator Hans Holzer explores true accounts of the strange and unknown: telepathy, psychic and reincarnation dreams, survival after death, psycho-ecstasy, unorthodox healings, Pagans and Witches, and Ufonauts. Reports included in this volume:

- Mrs. F. dreamed of a group of killers and was particularly frightened by the eyes of their leader. Ten days later, the Sharon Tate murders broke into the headlines. When Mrs. F. saw the photo of Charles Manson, she immediately recognized him as the man from her dream

- How you can use four simple "wish-fulfillment" steps to achieve psycho-ecstasy—turning a negative situation into something positive

- Several true accounts of miraculous healings achieved by unorthodox medical practitioners

- How the author, when late to meet with a friend and unable to find a telephone nearby, sent a telepathic message to his friend via his friend's answering service

- The reasons why more and more people are turning to Witchcraft and Paganism as a way of life

- When UFOs land: physical evidence vs. cultists

These reports and many more will entertain and enlighten all readers intrigued by the mysteries of life ... and beyond!

0-87542-368-X, 304 pp., mass market   **$4.95**